INSTITUTIONAL FREEDOM

A Collection of African American Studies Essays

Joy Elan

ISBN: 1500533599
ISBN 13: 9781500533595
Library of Congress Control Number: 2014912987
CreateSpace Independent Publishing Platform
North Charleston, South Carolina

DEDICATION

I dedicate this book to my family, my teachers, and my daughter. Every one of you inspired me to keep going and share my voice.
Jada, mommy will never stop writing and I don't want you to give up on anything you want to do! I love you, baby.

ACKNOWLEDGEMENT

I want to acknowledge the professors in the African American Studies Department at University California, Berkeley when I was attending there. I still apply what I learned to my life every day and that is the greatest gift of knowledge. Thank you for teaching and we need the African American Studies Department because it is a crucial part of United States' history.

TABLE OF CONTENTS

INTRODUCTION

It has been ten years since I have graduated from University California, Berkeley, and I miss those days. I miss being in a classroom with other students who voiced their opinions and were hungry to learn and change the world. I was one of them. As an African American student at University California, Berkeley from July 2001 through August 2004 (I graduated in three years), I experienced various forms of discrimination, either because of my disability, gender and most of all, my race. However, I did not allow that to stop me. I knew what I wanted and that was to go to University California, Berkeley and graduate. That was my dream since I was six years old, and my mother always told me I had to earn it.

I was born in a hospital in Berkeley, California but raised in Oakland. I moved to Berkeley for a few months but stayed in schools in Berkeley while residing in Oakland. My elementary, middle, and high schools surrounded University California, Berkeley's campus. I took it as a sign that it was meant for me to go there since I was getting closer to the campus every time I moved to a different school.

I attended Berkeley High School from fall 1997 until fall 2001, which was very diverse but separate. I was a floater. I got along with everyone and did not really have a clique. Berkeley High School was one of the few high schools in America to have an African American Studies Department. I took pretty much every course I could from 10th to the 12th grade in the African American Studies Department. We watched films and read literature that we probably would not have done in other general education courses. The discussions in classes were intense, and it made me hungry to learn more. I was exposed to so much history I would not have gotten elsewhere. I went to summer school to get general education requirements done so I could take other African American classes that were offered during the school year. Going to summer school helped me graduate a semester early, and I went back in June to walk the stage and get my diploma.

I believe in challenging the norm because I am not normal. I graduated from high school a semester early because I believed in "work now and play later." I loved to learn, and I was taught by my family that there is no such thing as "I can't." My family was from Louisiana, and they dealt with tougher things than I did. If they graduated from college and became teachers and other professions, then there was no excuse why I could not do the same thing. I thank my family for their support because I know it was not easy raising a disabled child when the odds seemed like they were against me.

During my semester off from high school and waiting to be accepted to University California, Berkeley, I took a semester of English at the community college, which was called Vista at the time, but now it is known as Berkeley City College. I wanted to improve my writing and prepare myself for college life. Six months without school was too long for me, and I had to stay busy. In April 2001, I got my acceptance letter to University California, Berkeley. After years of hearing teachers say I would not make it to University California, Berkeley, I made it. It is sad because their reasons were because I had hearing loss, and I was Black, and I did it! I was the first in my family not to go to Southern University; I wanted to see if I could get into one of the hardest universities on my merit. I bragged to all the teachers that said I would not make it. One teacher still said to go to San Francisco State University and I said, "Why? I made it into my dream school!"

I had to attend a Summer Bridge program to go to University California, Berkeley as part of the requirement to be admitted in the fall. It was an interesting summer; I had to stay in the dorm and participate in group activities with other students in the program. Most of the students were people of color, with mostly Latinos and Asians being the majority in the program. I took Political Science and an introductory course of Statistics. I passed Summer Bridge and was ready to start the fall. Attending the program helped me prepare for what college life was about and the first semester, I took a few courses in African American Studies. Since I completed the English class while I was waiting to get my diploma, I only needed one more English class to be done with my English requirement. I completed that my freshmen fall semester. I knew I wanted to take more African American Studies courses, so African American Studies would be my major.

I took African American Studies courses in the summer and all year around. I had a year of classes with one professor who had stimulating discussions and essay topics. He welcomed any essay topic as long as we had evidence to back up our statements. His teachings reminded me of the classes I had at Berkeley High. In fact, his last name was the same as my teacher at Berkeley High, but they were not related. He would always end his lessons with, "So what are you going to do about it?" He was empowering us and telling us what was the point of all this talking if we were not going to use it in our community. I loved his teaching style and wrote some of my best papers in his classes.

African American Studies removed the requirement of the thesis course to graduate during my junior year. Writing the thesis became a requirement for only students with honors. My professor encouraged us to take the thesis course because he said the thesis course would help us if we wanted to pursue graduate school. I knew I wanted to go to graduate school, and I wanted all the skills needed to excel. I did not have the GPA to take the honors thesis, but I requested the department to create a course number for me to take the regular thesis course since I was the only student interested in writing a thesis.

When it was time to write my thesis, I took some education and family life classes. My thesis topic focused on education and life; therefore, I took a couple of Sociology courses in the summer of 2003. My favorite professor from the African American Studies Department transferred to another college prior to my senior year and was not my thesis advisor. I worked with another professor who I heard wonderful things about and enjoyed working with him. I had a wonderful experience working with someone different. My thesis was about African Americans and Education, and he helped me narrow it down to talking about a topic that I could relate to: African American Deaf Education (this is included in the book). I asked him what the difference was in having a Master's degree and a PhD degree. He told me that with a Master's, I could teach community college and with a PhD, I could teach university. Becoming a professor at a university became my new goal, so I was determined to go for it. I completed my thesis and graduated in 2004.

I was determined to get my PhD in Education since I took Education courses at University California, Berkeley, and it became my minor, especially since it was related to my thesis. I learned that my passion was teaching, and I came from a family of teachers. I went to Stanford University: School of Education and completed my Master's program in one year, 2006-2007. I applied for the PhD programs twice since I graduated and was denied. I applied to teach at different community colleges and was denied. In the meantime, I wrote two poetry books and published them while trying to get a teaching position somewhere. In the spring of 2013, I was accepted to teach at Ohlone Community College. I taught there for one year in the Deaf Studies program and was laid off (welcome to the life of an adjunct professor).

While teaching at Ohlone, my supervisor informed that I was going to be teaching Deaf students Basic English grammar and reading while signing in American Sign Language. I was excited about the first day of school and being able to teach. I told my students about my background and how I did not want to hear any excuses. They were deaf and could not believe their teacher was a young African American woman with hearing aids. I told them I was their teacher, but they were mine too. I incorporated my favorite professor's teaching style in my classes to empower them. It was about them, not me. I missed being in the academic environment, and I enjoyed it so much. Some of them wanted to transfer to a four year degree, and I encouraged them to.

To remind myself how I was at their age, I went back to read a copy of my personal statement letter to University California, Berkeley.

While reading it, I read things that I spoke into existence in my future. I wrote poems about the African American struggle, my struggle, and I knew I spoke of those things in college. I pulled out my old floppy disks (remember those) and selected a few essays I wrote in different classes with my favorite professor. I noticed things I said then, I rephrased them into my poetry and those things I spoke about then are happening now. Two of my popular poems I wrote in my latest poetry book, *Silence Is Not Always Golden: A Poetic Revolution*, were *I'm A Survivor* and *Institutional Freedom*. *I'm A Survivor* was an African American history poem starting from the Trans-Atlantic slave trade until 2012, the year of the re-election of President Barack Obama. *Institutional Freedom* was about me having two degrees and having a hard time finding employment because I was overqualified (they are presented in this chapter a little later).

I talked about those things in my essays, and I wanted to show where I got my poetry themes from. I wrote a lot of relevant papers, and I thought about publishing them. I am a writer and poetry was my therapy. However, I have always been academic, and I still want to pursue my PhD one day. I know I have to publish research papers and books when I am a professor, but I do not have to wait to become a professor to publish. I published two poetry books; so, it is not hard.

The papers I put in my collection ranges from when I was seventeen to twenty, almost twenty-one years old. They are opinions and not facts. I quoted people to support my claims, but it was simply me voicing my opinions. Some were short like articles and some were long because they were research papers. The first chapter is my personal statement so people can understand my background and why I think the way I think. The rest are papers where I was passionate about the topic, and I felt I supported my claims. I got A's and B's on those papers. I received those grades because the professors understood what I was saying. The last chapter is my thesis paper, and I chose to end it that way because it was the finale to me graduating and closing that chapter in my University California, Berkeley life. I removed my professors' names to keep confidentiality.

I kept the essays the same. I did not want to change anything about what I wrote. It would be defeating the purpose of showing my progress and thought process back then. I did edit the grammar, but my statements are the same. I kept my legal name on my papers since that was who I was in college, but I am publishing by my author name to eliminate confusion. I thought about doing this after reading Angela Davis' book, *The Meaning of Freedom: And Other Difficult Dialogues*, where she published a collection of speeches. That is why the essays are revolved around African American Studies. There are different topics in the African American Studies courses that are similar and different. I used to end my papers in an optimistic tone, and as I gradually wrote more papers I ended it with a tone as "this is what happened and it needs to change." I am sharing this information because I read so many books and sometimes people were uninterested in what I read. Therefore, I discussed them in my essays and referred to them so the readers can read the books for themselves. .

Before I start with my personal statement, I want to give you the foundation of this book. I listed my essays by course numbers and the dates within each course. It gives people a chance to see my progression from what I learned in one course and transferring that information to another course. Some may seem similar, but the readings and statements will differ. These were the courses I took and these are the course descriptions from the African American Studies, Sociology, and Ethnic Studies Departments listed on the University California, Berkeley department websites. After those sections are the two poems that show what I learned from these courses and how they apply to my life now.

<u>AAS R1B</u>: Training in expository, argumentative, and other styles of writing. The assignments will focus on themes and issues in African American life and culture.

<u>AAS 5A:</u> African American Life and Culture in the United States: A study of the genesis, development, and scope of African American culture, approached through an examination of selected art forms, historical themes, and intellectual currents.

<u>AAS 5B:</u> African American Life and Culture in the United States: An interdisciplinary approach designed to help students understand the forces and ideas that are influencing the individual and collective African American experience.

<u>AAS 100:</u> Introduction to African American Studies: This course, lets students explore the status of African American studies as a discipline. The class will discuss the social relevance of African American studies, the political origins of the discipline, and the debate over Afrocentricity. Special attention will be devoted to the contributions of black feminist theory and community scholars/organic intellectuals to the development of the discipline.

<u>AAS 122:</u> African American Families in American Society: Examines the historical roles and functions of families in the development of black people in America from slavery to the present.

<u>AAS 159:</u> Special Topics in African American Literature Special topics in African American literature.

<u>Soc. 111 Sociology of the Family</u>: This course explores the social importance of families and dimensions of contemporary family life in the United States. We cover the history of families from the 19th century to today, focusing on the influence of marriage as a social institution and changes in family organization over time. We discuss differences in family patterns related to class and race and sociological theories about families, including gender socialization. Much of the course is devoted to exploring contemporary family life, including relationships between men and women; parents and children; the influence of the marketplace; and work and family.

<u>ES N144 (ES 144AC) Racism & the Law</u>: Intensive history-legal survey of racism in the United States, exploring the legal antecedents of the country's contemporary stratified society, and emphasizing the role of law as a social policy instrument. Readings and lectures will investigate the prevailing legal currency of racism in the United States through an examination of the country's formative legal documents

and the consequent effects of a myriad of judicial decisions on peoples of color.

ES 147 Women of Color in the U.S: Examines the history and contemporary situations of Chicana/Latina, African American, Asian American and Native American Women. Conceptual focus will draw on lived experiences and theoretical constructs of race, class and gender.

Here are the two poems that are a summary of what I learned and who I am.

I'm A Survivor

I'm a survivor of the Trans-Atlantic and Trans-America slave trade
I'm a product and survivor of rapes during slavery
No choice but to carry my babies into this horrible world
My babies being ripped from my uterus and arms
My "husband" auctioned off or lynched for rebelling
I know that because of my skin complexion
I was working in the house
Saying, "Yes master" and acting like I was his loyal subject
Yes, his loyal subject, subject to all kinds of abuse
While taking care of his family,
I'm learning how to read and write
Or listen to his conversations to warn the others
While I wash his clothes outside and pass by the other slaves
I sing "Wade in the Water"
To communicate to the others
That the water is the key to freedom
I'm a survivor of slaves learning how to read and write
At night, my work is never done
I teach others how to read and write
But teach them how to hide it
So we don't lose the battle to freedom
Southern trees bore strange fruits
And even though they're not growing in front of us
They're growing in someone's backyard
I'm a survivor of the Civil Rights Movement,
And dogs attacking me just because I want to vote
I'm a product and survivor of the Black Power Movement
Black Panther Party, "Power to the People"
Police brutality and FBI instigations/ infiltrations
Our leaders dying for a cause
And two rappers on two coasts used to cause a war
Within our own community
They say the best way to hide something from us
Is by putting it in a book
After all the things I went through to teach us how to read and write
in slavery

These two things, which are free, are becoming useless in our community
I'm proud to be from Oakland and Berkeley
Two cities that represent change and revolution
I'm Black, not African American
I don't identify with Africans because
I don't know what tribe or region I'm from
Because of the one drop rule,
I don't know who I was at first
I refuse to call myself an American because
I don't want to call myself something where the country doesn't even
want me
They keep finding ways to keep me oppressed or extinct
We fought to have a right to vote and the moment that we earned it,
People aren't registering or getting out there
Our rights to vote and freedom may be taken away
Because we're complacent and we don't know that
A war is going to break out in our own country
Just to put us back in slavery
We've been experiencing institutional slavery and racism
For the past 50 years
But it's about to get real just because we have a Black President
And he's not backing down
They're afraid that he's going to change America for the better
And they can't have that
It's getting tougher and tougher for us to vote
And express ourselves
There may be 99% of us but that 1% controls everything
I'm a fighter and I refuse to give up
I learned from all of these people that fought for us to be here today
Dead or alive; we have a right to live freely
I'm a survivor of all of these things because my ancestors
Made this country and we're being erased out of its history
Pick up a book and learn about the struggles that people went through
Just for us to be here today
I refuse to let all the movements
And those that laid down their life, die in vain

Institutional Freedom

I'm a prisoner of an institution
Not the prison system
But institution of higher learning
They got me tied down and bound
I can't be free
They keep coming after me financially
Even with the degrees
Jobs and businesses don't take me seriously
They look at my resume
And toss it to the side
You could've sworn that they
Saw that I went to San Quentin or some penitentiary
They saw two rival prestigious universities
And they asked me, "Who do you represent?"
I didn't go to them schools for the sports
You act like I'm in a gang and I have to claim turf
I proudly wear my school shirts
But I might as well be wearing
Prison identification numbers
In actuality, I'm in the same boat
As the person that went to prison
Thing is, they'll pick them before me
Just because they can pay them way less
How is it that I'm competing for the same jobs
With ex-cons and I was told that my education is the key
Key to what?!
Being treated like I did something wrong
Yeah, I peeped that I was the bottom 1% at them schools
Only 20-50 of us graduating out of a couple of thousands?
Now these jobs looking at me like I didn't earn my papers
Like the schools were doing me a favor letting me graduate
They're working together to keep me tied down and bound
That's what they are: institutions
Keeping me a prisoner in another form

They don't have control over my mind
I'm Andy Dufresne
Slowly chipping away at the wall
If it takes me 5, 10, 20 years to get out
So be it!
I'm not a Dumas (dumbass)
they don't know that I have a plan
Not to be a prisoner of a company
Nobody's gonna be telling me when to eat, sleep, work
.They'll keep transferring me from prison to prison
Until I'm old enough to collect social security
And all that hard work was just a waste of my life
When I'm out, I'm gonna be so long gone
And chilling with hella paper
I'm young enough to break free
And do as I please!

*Reference from Shawshank Redemption

Institutional Freedom is one of my favorite poems because the title alone represents everything I stand for: freedom from being institutionalized. I am a teacher all the time, and I do not believe in academic classrooms as being the only learning space. As I learned at University California, Berkeley, democracy and education is one of the best teaching tools. It is giving students a chance to challenge the way they have been taught. I used this method when I taught at Ohlone, and I am presenting this to you to show you how to think outside the box. As I have said before, silence is not always golden, and I definitely think knowledge should always be shared. The readers may not agree with what I said, but I ask people to keep an open mind while reading my work. After all, we are all students in this world, and I am constantly learning and evolving.

There was a shirt the African American students at University California, Berkeley used to wear. It was black, and the letters on the front were white and it read: "represent." On the left sleeve it read: "University California, Berkeley." On the back it read: "Less than 3.9%." Another shirt had different percentages decreasing over time and one year read, "2008: You do the math." This is me representing the African American Studies Department and African American student body at University California, Berkeley. Sharing my essays is me doing something about it.

HEAR THE WORLD THROUGH MY EARS (PERSONAL STATEMENT TO UNIVERSITY CALIFORNIA, BERKELEY)

The old gym, dark and gloomy with the lights flickering above me as if they could blow out any minute; outside, an overcast day with the sounds of the football players practicing for their next game; inside, squeaky sneakers running and the sounds of girls laughing. Here I am at cheerleading practice, in the back and center of the chaos.

"Places, ladies," my coach mumbles. "Joy, I want you to do this routine. "Her voice drifts away into a blurry sound. The cheerleaders were talking in a huge crowd. I was straining to lip-read and hear my coach's instructions. I thought I understood, but I did not. I moved to the wrong place, and suddenly everyone was on the floor laughing hysterically at me. I looked across the gym and saw my coach's face. She let out a frustrated groan and rolled her eyes at me. She threw her hands up like she had lost hope, then mockingly moved her hands to imitate sign language. I was boiling with anger, and I felt a wave of tears pushing against my eyes.

As I grew up, the issue of my hearing loss became important in school. Teachers who did not believe in me thought I would fall behind in a "regular" classroom, and I would not be able to understand what was going on. I became skilled at speaking and lip-reading. However, in the classroom, it was too much of a struggle to understand what the teachers were saying over the background noises of the students. Fortunately, I could keep up with the use of a skilled sign language interpreter.

Wearing hearing aids have allowed me to achieve in and out of school. To me, they are like glasses, helping to bring clarity to the world around me. To others, they are alien-like, and something they can tease me about because they do not understand. I wear my hair down to avoid people's stares. When they see my hearing aids, their mouths tend to drop because all along they thought I was "normal." I like to challenge people's perceptions and force them to accept me for who I am.

The cheerleading experience has taught me not everyone is mature enough to accept other people's differences. But in the end, I have shown people that my hearing loss does not stop me from reaching my goals, and it has encouraged me. I have achieved a great deal and I will continue to overcome the challenges that will face me, in the future.

Joy Sledge
Af Am R1B
9-17-01

CORPORATE MEDIA VS. INDEPENDENT MEDIA

Independent media is when the news is based off of opinion, and it does not have a lot of sponsors. I do not know if the corporate media is correct or if the independent media is, but all I do know is they tell the news how they see it. The independent media talks about how the corporate media gives people negative images of what is going on in the world. Now people are having bad ideas of other races and ethnicities because the corporate media presents the images, and people believe them. The corporate media is a powerful impact in today's society due to the fact that people will do and believe anything they see on television.

I have never seen independent media until recently, and their news were similar to the one seen on television. Everyone was talking about the war or if there was really going to be one and the independent media brought up some good suggestions; such as, how was the United States going to war without knowing who really committed the terrorist attack. The corporate media was talking about how they knew who it was by looking at the people in the other countries. Just because the other countries were happy did not mean they had something to do with the crime. I could be happy that Bush was not president but that does not mean I voted him out; I was not able to vote at the time.

When I saw the people in the other countries cheering about the attack, I was furious and hurt because the media presented the image of those few people who were celebrating. I wanted something bad to happen to those people who were happy, but I could not because they were in their own country. They were a few people out of so many. The corporate media had so much power to make things horrible or pleasurable because they were paid to be biased and encourage everyone else to think the same way. The independent media helped me to see things from a different perspective. I was tired of seeing the same opinion on every channel the news was on. I think I could agree with the other countries if they hate America. Sometimes I hate this country myself. The racism in our own country has made us act the same way with the other countries, and the corporate media wants everyone to stand together until the war is over. The media can be confusing on how they want people to be, but if we are supposed to stand together, why can't we stand together forever? That is why we have the independent media. They give a broader understanding of things, and they are not hypocritical.

I do not know who sponsors the corporate media, but I do know they have to be sponsored if they are on cable and everyone can watch what is going on. Even though both media corporations are giving out the same information, people still do not know who is telling the truth and who is exaggerating the truth. But the only way we will know is if we hear the people speak for themselves, such as hearing the president declare a war against the terrorists. There is no contest between both media corporations. They have different opinions, so it is up the public to decide which one to listen to.

Joy Sledge
AAS 5A
3-7-02

FRIENDSHIP WITH THE OPPOSITE SEX

What is a friend to you: someone who helps you through the hard times or someone who is there for the good times? Maybe both. Zora Neale Hurston depicted the importance of friendship between a man and a woman in her book, *Their Eyes Were Watching God*. She demonstrated this with Janie and her husband, Tea Cake. Janie was a Black woman who wanted to be independent, and she wanted to live her life the way she wanted to. Tea Cake was one of Janie's friends who supported her and who she shared her life with. They shared the experiences of life and reality as Black people. Through the good and bad times, they stuck together to laugh at it later.

In the middle of the book, Hurston showed how Janie's friendship with Tea Cake was a powerful influence in Janie's life as she shared her companionship with a male. Their friendship was initiated by a friendly game of checkers.

> "How about playin' you some checkers? You looks hard tuh beat" . . . He set it up and began to show her and she found herself glowing inside. Somebody wanted her to play. Somebody thought it natural for her to play. That was even nice" (95-96).

Tea Cake was showing Janie how to play checkers and that was a new idea to her since Janie's last two husbands did not want her to do anything. This scene was important because their friendship was beginning and as a friend, Tea Cake was telling her she was free to do anything she wanted to. Janie saw she was independent to do anything she was willing to do and that was why she glowed when he invited her to play with him. This showed how Black people can have fun with each other without knowing who they were socializing with. Tea Cake was nearly 20 years younger than Janie, but that showed that age did not matter. It was the person's personality that attracted you and how they present themselves to you. When it comes to men and women being friends in the Black life, you help or support each other and try to have a good time. It does not have to be serious, just a good time to relax and look back. As Janie and Tea Cake's friendship bloomed, their relationship did also. Their relationship turned into husband and wife, which made their bond stronger.

Their friendship and relationship with one another helped get them through the hard times, such as the time when they were stuck in a hurricane, near the end of the book. While trying to evacuate to a safe area, they nearly died and worried about trying to survive. They left a friend in an abandoned house fearing the house would blow down, and they would die. When the hurricane was over, and they were safely in another town Tea Cake said:

"Who you reckon Ah seen, Janie? Bet you can't guess."

" . . . Ah g'wan and tell me, Tea Cake. Ah don't know. It can't be Motor Boat."

"Dat's jus' who it is. Ole Motor! De son of a gun laid up in dat house and slept and de lake come moved de house way off somewhere and Motor didn't know nothin' bout it till de storm wuz 'bout over . . . Yeah man. Heah we nelly kill our fool selves runnin' way from danger and him lay-up dere and sleep and float on off" (173).

This moment shows even though they went through a lot of trouble to be safe, they were able to laugh about it in the end. They were laughing because they risked their lives in the hurricane when all they had to do was stay in the house and still be alive. That was how Black people's lives were; they came to a point in their lives where they had to make choices. There was no telling what will happen but they tried to do what they could do to be safe. No matter what the outcome was if they had good friends, they were able to share their pain or happiness with them. Knowing they could have died, they were not paranoid about what happened to them. What mattered was they were still together to laugh and reflect on the incident. Their relationship as husband and wife made their friendship stronger and secured because they were able to talk to one another about anything.

These examples showed how in the Black society, men and women stuck together no matter what the problem was. If a child asked their mother something, the mother said to the child, "Let me talk to your father about it." This type of communication showed the partnership of the parents and their relationship with one another. No one was left out in making the decision, and they shared the roles. My grandparents were a close couple. They knew each other since high school, and they had a special bond with one another. They raised their children together, and they made sure their children went to college. Both of them had jobs and were equal to one another. Equality was important in the Black society; we had control of what happened in our family. No one could be separated anymore, and we were able to provide for each other. In order to do so, we had to stick together and support each other. Those examples were important because as man and wife you must be supportive and work together as a team. If you are not friends before lovers, then the relationship can break apart because your trust in one another is not there.

Hurston pointed out the importance of unity because without it there was no community. Tea Cake and Janie were a good example of how Black relationships were and should be in this time period. People jumped into relationships without knowing who they were with and did not set up a foundation to make the relationship strong. Friendship is important between a man and a woman because you can set up trust and that will keep your relationship strong. Even if there is no relationship between the two, the friendship is just as good. In true friendship, you are able to share things with one another and help each other out in terms of the opposite sex's point of view.

Joy Sledge
AAS 159
6-26-02

TEENA MARIE AND HER SUCCESS IN BLACK MUSIC

"Baby, what's happening, entre vous Lady Tee. I've heard a boat-load of other ladies' raps but they ain't got nothing on me... I've been called Casper, Shorty, Lil' Bit and some they call me Vanilla Child..." This line is heard in Teena Marie's "Square Biz." Teena Marie was a singer and the queen of funk, who happened to be white. Her voice was strong and authentic. If you have never seen her, you would think she was Black. She was a successful white female artist that was embraced in the African American community. "Other white R&B singers have been briefly accepted by black radio and fans. Teena is the only one to be totally embraced" (*Lovergirl: the Teena Marie Story*, album). Also, stated in *Behind the Groove: Unofficial Teena Marie Page*:

> "Though Teena is loved by her fans of all races, it is especially significant to note how widely she is accepted in the black community as "one of their own" because of her soulful music. She is authentic and real and it shows in her music and voice".

Teena Marie was one of the first females to accomplish many obstacles in the music industry and opened doors to many music artists today. Her life has shown how hard she worked to make her dreams come true and how true artists are rewarded for the hard work they put into their work or projects.

She was born as Mary Christine Brockert (Teena Marie is a flip of her first and middle names) on March 5, 1956. Teena lived in the San Fernando Valley before her family moved back to Venice Beach, when she was in the fifth grade. In Venice, it was a "multicultural community that contributed to Teena's musical foundation" (*I Need Your Lovin', The Very Best of Teena Marie*, album). Her older brother liked hard rock, and turned her onto some of the artists such as Janis

Joplin and Jimi Hendrix. Her older sister was a Motown fan, and her other sister was into pop music. She also had musical influences from her parents, which she loved such artists such as Frank Sinatra, Sarah Vaughan and Lena Horne and "from the Hispanic families in the neighborhood came a love for Latin music" (*I Need Your Lovin'*). With all of these different music tastes, she combined them and made it into her own style. The Latin beats can be heard in her song "Portuguese Love" and the pop can be heard in "Lovergirl." The Sarah Vaughan and Lena Horne style can be heard in some of her jazz songs such as "Casanova Brown," where she sings and plays the piano. However, it took some time for Teena to play her style for her audience, but it was worth the time and struggle.

Teena Marie overcame a huge obstacle in the music industry for the Black audience. In 1975, the founder of Motown records, Berry Gordy, discovered her. It took some time for her first album to come out because she was busy working on other projects. The interesting thing about Teena Marie was her work was full of wonders, and it was original. Music artists copy her work as some rap artists sample her beats and her lyrics, such as Fugees, Master P and Snoop Dogg and others. In the mid-1800s, White people were known for copying Black people's dances and music and claiming that they created it. It was either to mock the African Americans or steal the African American's creativity. In *African American Jazz and Rap*, by James L. Conyers, Jr., he states on page 181:

> "Even though, White supremacy became a tool of oppression, Whites were always drawn to and fascinated by the creative ethos of African peoples... The minstrel tradition, with its pejorative and grotesque images, was both an attempt by Whites to copy Black creative expression and to preserve White supremacy... Talented Black performers were associated with recorded music from the inception of the industry, but Whites gained greater success through performing Black music."

African Americans did not like White people taking their music and dances and when it became mainstreamed; they created something new to call their own. African Americans had a hard time selling records during the mid- 1900s because White people were not willing to buy Black music. In order to sell a record, Black people's faces were not on album covers. They did not want people to know they were Black. Instead, they would use White faces or no faces because they wanted the audience to decide on the music and not the skin color; this was the opposite for Teena Marie.

In 1979, when her first album came out, Motown did not put her picture on the cover because they were afraid that Black people would not buy it. They were afraid that Blacks would think she was another White person trying to be Black and steal their music, which is R&B. In the *Behind the Groove: The Unofficial Teena Marie Page* it states that:

> "On her first album *Wild & Peaceful,* Motown didn't feature any pictures of her on the album jacket, afraid that people may not buy the record if they knew she was white. (This is a reversal of many record company practices in the 50s and 60s. They would place pictures of whites or "generic" scenes on the covers of records by black artists because the companies were scared that whites wouldn't buy albums with blacks on the front)."

Also, she said on VH-1's *Where Are They Now: Girl Power*, that in 1979, "they did not put her picture on her first album because at that time, they didn't think people would understand." "Motown had confidence in her talent, but wondered whether their mainly Black audience would accept the funky Caucasian... But by the time people saw Teena in person, it was too late; they loved her" (*Where Are They Now*). On her second album, the front and back covers featured her picture, and she continued to sell because she won over the Black audience. Also, when she performed she said, "there would be 17,000 people in the audience and the majority of them were Black" (*Where Are They Now*). The fact that she was accepted in the African American community because of her music and not her skin color was a huge breakthrough in music. She was not KC and the Sunshine band, a group that did disco music, which was only a phase, but she did R&B music, which has been around for a few decades and will continue to be around.

One of her good friends and mentor was Rick James. He taught her many things about the music business, such as how to produce and to be independent. They were a team; he helped produce her first album, and he sang duets with her. When it was time to do her second album, he told her she could do it on her own. But still unconvinced of her abilities, Teena asked Richard Rudolph, the late Minnie Riperton's husband, to produce her second album. By her third album, she was writing and producing her own material; she was one of the few women to write and produce her own songs at the time.

Teena Marie's music was selling, and she was nominated for the Grammy's a few times. She lost to Aretha Franklin and a few other female artists. Her music was crossing over from R&B to pop, but she was still an R&B artist first before a pop artist (instead of being pop artist first crossing over to R&B). Even though her music was selling, Teena was not getting paid a lot of money. She sued Motown in 1982 for nonpayment of royalties (*Behind the Groove*, website). She did not want to record for them anymore due to the fact that she had a bad contract. "Teena did not want to record for them anymore due to her bad recording contract (negotiated while she was still a minor, and signed without being allowed benefit of legal counsel) and not getting paid..." (*Behind the Groove*, website). Teena also has a law named after her called the "Teena Marie Bill," passed by US Congress, and it is still in effect today. "The bill states a label cannot legally keep an artist contractually bound if they refuse to release their records. It also establishes that an artist under contract must be paid at least $6,000 per year" (*Behind the Groove*). Teena left Motown for Epic records and continued to sell music.

When Teena went to Epic, she had "her biggest pop and R&B hits" (Teena Marie: Ultimate Collection, album). Teena had hits such as "Lovergirl" and "Ooo La La La," which brought out her musical abilities. In "Lovergirl," she is seen playing the guitar, which she played as if it was a rock song and "Ooo La La La," showed her sensual side that made people fall in love with the song. "Ooo La La La" did not win her a Grammy, but the Fugees won a Grammy for the remake of the song some years later. She said they used the melody and some of the lyrics and asked her to sing in the sample (*Where Are They Now*). She left Epic a little after 1990 and established her own record, Sarai Records. She had one album out on her independent label, but it was not in stores long enough for people to capture it. Some independent labels do not make enough business if they do not have the proper legal properties to keep something in the market. However, that one album/ compact disc can be bought off her website: www.teenamarie.com. She is currently working on another album called *Black Rain*, which should be coming soon now that she was able to have a record deal to make sure she did not make the same mistake with the other album. She said on her official Website, September 9, 2001 (exact wording):

> "Hi Yall, I'm still working on Black Rain. I'm not fee-lin some of the tunes, I want all the tunes on this CD to reflect my message, spiritually and emotionally. I don't have to do a CD because the record company needs this or that, I'm doing this because I am an artist. I just want to ex-por-ess myself as a singer- songwriter by bringin whats in my heart to y'all."

Her message to her fans showed how much she was devoting her time to her music; she was a true artist and not some artist that are here and then you do not hear from them again.

Teena Marie has shown what can happen when you put your mind to it. Her songs are always played on radio stations such as KISS FM, KBLX, KMEL and Wild 94.9. She continued to go on tour, and she could still sell out a concert. Her performance was one you would not want to miss. She was the first female to have a rap on a record and to produce her own music. In conclusion, Teena stated: "It didn't matter what color my skin was, my audience came because they loved the music. That's pretty amazing. That is a blessing and it brought me to my knees many, many times" (*Where Are They Now*).

Joy Sledge
AAS 5B
9-27-02

THE CONFRONTATIONS WITHIN THE FREE AFRICAN AMERICAN COMMUNITY

African Americans have always had different perspectives of how to improve their community so future African Americans could advance their status on the social ladder. James Oliver Horton and Lois E. Horton discussed in their book, *In Hope of Liberty*, the different obstacles free African Americans faced to improve their community in the North. Prior to the Civil War, free African Americans were finding new ways to help each other out, such as providing jobs and donating money to lower class African Americans.

There were a variety of opinions of how to approach the issues in the African American community. Three of the issues discussed in the book ultimately lead to disagreements, which a few people had to go their own separate ways to form their own group. One of the issues was women forming their own party to deal with the social issues that were important to them, as opposed to staying with the men's party. Secondly, a conflict between men and women was when a growing interest in women longed to preach.

Women had to form their own church once some men disapproved of female preachers. The final conflict was centered on the African-born people who were trying to encourage African American people to return to Africa rather than stay in America. It was the notion that American Americans should not stay in a country where they were not wanted. These three encounters were huge impacts that effected how African Americans live today.

A few years before the turning of the 19th century, African American men had formed their own groups, aside from the White men. Their purpose of separating from the White community was to establish a graveyard and build a church that served only Black people. At the same time, there were women in the group who felt they did not only want to establish a graveyard or a church, but services that would help other African Americans as well.

At the bottom of page 127 to the top of page 128, it said, "The reason for separate groups was probably a complex combination of cultural heritage, gender discrimination, and gender affinity." Women's views of improving the African American community were different from the men's views, and it was best for them to form their own groups and look at new areas that needed to be improved. Without the influence of men, they could work better. If it were all women, with the use of their intelligence they could figure out the problems that needed to be solved. Furthermore, both genders could accomplish more to improve the community in different ways. The women donated money to lower class African Americans and participated in political discussions, which was unheard of for American women at the time. Women who formed their own parties showed independence and that they were superior beings with the men.

Not only were women forming their own benevolent groups, but also African American women were becoming preachers, aside from their male counterparts. Men did not approve of female preachers because preaching had always been a man's task. For example, many male preachers disapproved of one woman by the name of Julia Foote, because they did not like her "religious expression" (146). Foote "joined forces with three other women preachers who had also been opposed by the ministers and hired a hall for a series of religious meetings" (146-147). Women wanted to express how they felt about the Bible and about slavery; it was not just the men's jobs to serve the African American community or speak about the Bible. That was a conflict because men were used to being the superior being, and the women were supposed to be subservient to the men. Church was supposed to be a place for all people to go and ask God for guidance; if religion was for all colors then it was also for all genders. As long as people were saying good words about the Bible or the religion, then what difference did it make if it was a kid or a grownup; male and female? Women decided to take matters into their own hands and felt they could help their community, especially the African American women. With the women being in power, alongside with the men, African Americans were taught they could do anything they wanted, no matter what sex or race they were.

Since the free African Americans had the power to do almost anything they wanted, they had an option to go back to Africa. However, some African Americans did not feel they belonged to Africa since they were born in America, especially because they did not know the language and which country to go to. On page 178, it states:

"Many felt a connection to Africa based on racial heritage, but some had more direct ties . . . African Americans maintained a strong attachment to African culture, but they also participated in the American culture they helped to create."

To go back to a country, which they were not familiar with, was hard to determine if they should stay in an oppressive country or return "home." Yes, people's roots were in their native country, but at the same time African Americans had been mixed with different tribes to know where to go. Some of the African-natives here in America helped influenced many African American people to go back to their homeland. However, for those who were born in America felt they belonged here because they helped produce America. America would have been nothing but land if the Africans never cultivated it and grew crops.

That was a conflict within the African American community because people were from both sides of the water. It was an identity issue. It was okay to return to Africa if they wanted to do it, but if people were separated from somewhere or something for a long time, it was hard to adapt to the new area or substance because they were used to their old customs. If all the African Americans went to Africa then they would not be confronting the American system of inequality, they would be running away. For those that stayed, they opened doors for many African Americans and they made so much progress since they were brought here to America.

Thanks to the three conflicts, African American people have fought for their rights and for equality because people stood up for what they believed in. African American women started benevolent groups and became preachers because they wanted to express their rights and their minds. They did not want the men making all of the decisions; they wanted to help make decisions too. Then the people who wanted to remain in America instead of returning to Africa were courageous because they felt that they had an unfinished battle in America, which was to fight for equal rights and higher status. These three groups of people paved the way for African Americans today; we have lawyers, doctors, judges and etc. African American people have moved up the social ladder, and they are still not finished fighting the battle because there are still some injustices continuing between African Americans and the corporate world. The people who stood up for what they believed in made it easier for future African American people to stand up, and they taught them to never give up without a fight because in the end it will be all worth it.

Joy Sledge
AAS 5B
11-4-02

AFRICAN AMERICANS' LIVES IN THE NORTH

The post-Civil War era was a confusing time for African Americans in the North. When the Blacks were freed in the South, many migrated to the North to seek better jobs, educational opportunities, and better living conditions. Due to the fact the North was supposed to be better for African Americans, it really was not any better. African Americans were not granted the resources they thought they would obtain due to the lack of skills to work or competition with immigrants coming from European countries. In *Black Migration*, it discussed how the African Americans faced discrimination in the North as well as in the South, but they could not determine if the conditions in the North were better or worse. African Americans had to adapt to the North's living conditions but even that adaption had its negative and positive sides to it. The characteristics that have affected African American's adaptation in the North were economical and psychological. They had to have money to survive and a positive self-esteem to pursue better living conditions. At times, these two things were hard to maintain in the African American community.

In the chapter, *Life and Death in the Inner City*, it discussed the issues African American families had to face in order to survive in the urban North. One of the issues was how there were more African American women in the northern cities than African American men and how the women were mainly head of the households, instead of the men. On page 95, it said:

> "Yet there is no question but census takers found more black women than men in the northern ghettos, especially in New York, where they counted 810 men for every 1,000 women in 1890, 809 men for every 1,000 women in 1900..."

This emphasized the number of African American women who had to go to the North to seek employment so they could provide for their families. This was a positive thing for the African American women because there were not many jobs in the South. In the North they were paid more. Also, this was significant in the African American community because African American women became more independent, and they could try to improve their family life by trying to move up in the economy. Since there were a lot of African American women working in the urban ghettos, it aided their adaptation in the cities because they felt some comfort knowing someone else knows how it was to be the only one to provide for their families.

White women did not have to work, unless they were poor immigrants, but the fact that the African American women were the backbone for their families shows how dedicated they were to "put a roof over their heads and food on the table." However, without the men, there were some serious economic issues in the Black community. "Women were (or seemed to be) heads of households in more than 20 per cent of Chicago ghetto families... most of them were in domestic service, with long and irregular hours" (*Black Migration*, 99). Since there were not many men to help the women, the women had to work two jobs or work too many hours to provide food and clothes for their families. The strain this caused them was the negative part to the adaptation in the North; women were not used to working in factories or other jobs. The stress of working long hours in factories was hard for the women to be the only person taking care of the children. There was no one to watch the children and most of the time it was hard to put food on the table. The women thought their working hours were going to improve once they reached the North but realized how hard it was to survive without money to the point where they had to work irregular hours.

Families who had single mothers had to struggle to have a place to live, since their mothers were not making enough money. Another economic impact on the African Americans in the North was lodging with a few families in one small apartment or room. It "was a traditional ghetto means of boosting the family income" (*Black Migration*, 102). Since the rent was high for African Americans in the cities, as opposed to it being high for the Whites, African American people had to have roommates, so they could pay the rent and save a few dollars. This helped African American people adapt to the urban cities because people did not know anybody they could stay with until they found their own place. They had to adapt to this living condition because there was nowhere else they could go where they can have all the space they wanted; they had to save money in order to own their property. People could save their money to buy their own property if there were more people lodging with them. "... Landlords got $25 a month for flimsy one-story frame row houses that would have rented to Whites for $18" (102-103). This showed the exploitation of African Americans while they were trying to become stable in the North. With lodgers you could split the rent and people could pitch in so they could have money for other necessities. The bad part about having too many people lodging in a tight space was it became unsanitary and uncomfortable. "In the most crowded sections, beds were rented on a double-shift basis... More often than not, the sleeping space was damp, dark and airless. Water and toilets were usually out in the yard" (104). With this tight space, it was easier to become sick since there was no air and people had to go outside to use the bathroom or drink water. People had to accept the fact that a place to sleep was better than staying out on the streets. This affected their adaptation in a negative way because people were constantly getting sick and people were always trying to find another place to lodge that may have a bigger space. African Americans had to deal with this until they could afford a better place.

Single mothers and lodging with people had its negative and positive sides to it. However, lodging with multiple families affected how the children were raised in the ghettos. There was free education for the children in the North, and those who migrated to the urban cities went to school. School was one of the positive things for African Americans because they were able to learn to read and write. Adults from the South felt education meant power or freedom, and they forced their children to get an education. Schools did not help African Americans adapt to the North for long. When the children went to school they were mocked, and no one was willing to help them. "Many of them had never been to school at all, and even those who had were severely retarded by comparison with northern children, Black and White" (*Black Migration*, 98). These children were perceived as retarded people because of their lack of education and this had a negative impact on their adaptation in the North. It affected them psychologically and made them feel inferior. As stated later on in the chapter:

> "The schools were new and strange, and the academically retarded southern child got little help in adjusting to them; they felt inferior and tended to become 'incorrigibles,' then truants, and finally juvenile delinquents" (124).

Children who did not have mothers or people watching them constantly were the ones who got into the most trouble. They were "exposed to all the vice crime that flourished there, and many of them thrown on their own while their mothers worked, might be expected to get into trouble, and many did" (123). The lodgers could not help the children because they had their own problems to deal with. Since families had to lodge and there was not any space in the homes, the children did not have a place to play or any privacy. Also, because the schools made the children feel inferior and not welcome, that influenced many of the children to join gangs and stay in trouble to boost their confidence. That was probably why most of the children went to the streets because the streets made them feel "at home."

Urban cities were not very welcoming to many of the African Americans, and they turned their backs on the rural African Americans. Although there were supposed to be opportunities for African Americans, there really was not many opportunities for them. Many had to struggle to get an education, a job, and a place to stay until they were ready to be on their own. However, the North sort of caused more problems in the African American community instead of solving them. Children were joining gangs because the schools refused to help them, single mothers were working too many hours to feed their families, and people were lodging with strangers because they could not afford their own places. These were the negative sides that affected African Americans adaptation in the North. There were also some good things that helped African Americans feel welcomed in the North, and it all depended on the economic and the mentality of the person who wanted to succeed. If someone had a positive mentality, they were able to move up economically and socially and become more stable; they did not let anything or anyone hold them down. When they were constantly struggling to have better living conditions, they had a choice to keep doing what they were doing, until hopefully one day, it will all be worth it.

Joy Sledge
AAS 122
9-19-02

BLACK AUTHENTICITY

To have something to claim for yourself or your culture shows the significance of who you are. To be authentic means to be original and true to your culture and background. Black authenticity is no longer a Black cultural substance to Black people, and it never has been since slavery. Anything African Americans create does not stay within their community because other ethnicities tend to replicate African American creations, especially European Americans. It is hard for African Americans to come up with a new style or invention without European Americans trying to claim it and say they created the idea, such as braids, clothes style, and including music. White people have been replicating or mocking African Americans since the mid-1800s, before the Emancipation Proclamation.

In the mid-1800s, White people began to imitate African Americans in minstrel shows; they mocked the clothes, hairstyles, dialect, and facial expressions. However, the main thing they imitated and tried to claim at the same time was the music. In James L. Conyers book, *African American Jazz and Rap*, he stated:

> "Even though White supremacy became a tool of oppression, Whites were always drawn to and fascinated by the creative ethos of African peoples . . . The minstrel tradition, with its pejorative and grotesque images, was both an attempt by Whites to copy Black creative expression and to preserve White supremacy" (181).

White people stripped the Africans of their native language and customs; they wanted to make sure they had control over their "property." Since the Africans could not speak their native language, they had to adapt to the White people's language and customs. However, when the Africans or African Americans did adapt to White people's customs, they also combined some of the African customs into their lives and music. When they created something with a mixture of American culture and African culture, the White people felt they had to claim it or mock it, rather than strip the African Americans of their new customs. This process continued to happen up to the present day and most likely, will continue for years to come. Conyers stated how when the Black performer's recorded, White people tried to claim the music and say they did the music.

> "Talented Black performers were associated with recorded music from the inception of the industry, but Whites gained greater success through performing Black music. The fascination for Black life continued, but the formula by which White audiences could experience their version of Black culture through White performers became a lucrative one" (Conyers, 181).

White people took over many of the African American customs. Every time there was a new creation within the African American community, the White people took over the new creation (i.e., slang words, styles of clothing). African Americans created ragtime, country, blues, jazz, rock and roll, rhythm and blues (R&B), and rap. Out of all the music listed, White people took over country, rock and roll. There are many in blues and jazz. African Americans do not want to share their customs with the people who stripped away their identity and oppressed them for 200 years; they want something to call their own.

R&B, rap, and jazz seem to be still predominately Black music (although jazz is starting to be mainly White artists). There are at least one or two popular White people in each of these genres; Teena Marie is a popular white person in R&B, Eminem is popular in rap, and Kenny G and Paul Hardcastle are popular in jazz.

These four people (although there could be more people) are the only White people accepted in these genres of African American music because they are authentic and do not try to buy their way into the Black community. The African American community accepted these people as their own because they have proved that they are not fake, and they (maybe not Eminem) truly embrace the African American music legends from blues up to R&B. Teena Marie was inspired by different ethnicities and created her own style of R&B. Teena Marie is a phenomenal woman because she broke the barrier to be accepted in the Black community for R&B music. Berry Gordy, founder of Motown records, did not put her picture on her first album cover because he wanted his predominately Black audience to think she was Black. Her voice sounded like she was Black, but when people saw her face on the second album, they did not care that she was White; they liked her music.

Not many White artists were able to do that and if they did, they ended up crossing over to pop or rock music. This is important in the history of Black music because Black people are trying to be authentic, and it is hard when people try to steal your identity. They were tired (and they still are) of White people imitating and "stealing" their way of life. That is why they are very "strict" with White people who are trying to be an R&B or rap artist. Blacks do not want many of them trying to come in and take over what they started and kept going for a few decades.

Music is one of the aspects of Black authenticity because it comes from our culture and background. Every country has different types of music because of their resources and beliefs. There are other ways to describe Black authenticity, but music is an important factor; it creates clothes style and dances based on the beats and rhythm (you would not wear some nice tight pants to break dance in, you would wear pants that are loose so you can dance flexibly).

Without music in the African American community, the communication system is lost. African Americans rely on music to understand what to do when good or bad times occur. Black people create new genres of music when White people take over the other genres because they do not want the White people "speaking their language," similar to how White people did not want the Africans to read and write. Blacks want a communication system within their own community, not with the whole world. Also, that is another reason why slave songs such as, "Wade in the Water" were important to sing. There was a message within the song and that message was not meant for White people or other ethnicities to comprehend. Music has always been a part of African or African Americans' lives and will continue to be, if they can have their own music or language within their own community.

Joy Sledge
AAS 100
2-8-03

AFRICAN AMERICAN STUDIES AS A DISCIPLINE AND A DEPARTMENT

African American Studies is a very important subject to study. It is one aspect of American history, and it shows how America came about. As an African American student, my teachers never taught me how slavery existed when the Americans fought the British and when the Civil War occurred. I learned about slavery occurring during the Civil War when I was older, but my teachers never taught me when the first Africans arrived to America. They also never told the students about the different slave rebellions that happened between the Middle Passage and the Nat Turner revolt. Of course, I was told about Harriet Tubman and the Underground Railroad but that was mainly it. People do not know about how Africans/African Americans have resisted the notion of slavery and how the fruit of their labor helped make America prosperous. People think slaves picked cotton and served White people, but there is more to it. There is another culture within the slave/African American community.

Africans were stripped of their native customs and brainwashed to obey the White people. They had to have something to claim for their culture, such as using drums and singing. What the slaves did affected the future generations of African Americans, such as how Blacks play music, do their chores, and wear their clothes and hair. Those things have an impact on today's African Americans. I just finished studying about how Blacks went to jail after the Emancipation Proclamation and how Whites created laws to get Blacks in prison and use their labor for cheap wages or no wages at all. This signifies why there are more Blacks in jail today and how some things have not changed in over 100 years. When you compare the 1800's to the 1900's of the Black community, there are a lot of things that are related to one another. The 1860's changed things for the African Americans in terms of freedom and the 1960's meant Civil Rights; they were fighting for the same thing 100 years later. You can link a lot of things from the past to today's social issues, especially the political issues.

In two years at University California, Berkeley, I have learned a lot about African Americans (such as, how the Ku Klux Klan originated, slave rebellions, prisons, lodging and peonage, just to name a few). There is so much to learn about the African American way of life and a lot of people are ignorant of what African Americans went through. A teacher told me "Roots" was the first slave movie to show what slavery was about and how it looked. When I watched that movie, it was too clean for the White audience. I have seen slave movies where the actions and scene were too intense to watch. I know African Americans went through a lot because I am from that history. My grandparents and my mom told me about some of the racism they have experienced. A lot of White people do not know racism exist today. They think racism is segregation and "White"/ "Colored" signs. Segregation may not be visible, but racism is still visible, except it is more institutionalized. By taking African American courses, people can learn how racism has transformed in a 400 years period and see how it exists in the Black community and other communities as well (Jewish, Chicano/ Latino).

African American Studies should be a discipline and a department because there are a lot of resources people can use to study African Americans. People are still learning more about African Americans every day, discovering more information than before. If there is an American Studies Department or a History Department, then there should be an African American Studies Department as well. People know enough about American history, but there are other pieces of history to study too, such as Latino/ Chicano, Native Americans, Chinese, and etc. People should be open-minded and liberal to learn new things about other cultures and people. The earth is a big planet, and there is so much happening on earth that people only see what they want to see. Also, a lot of Black people do not know who they are and where they are from. Alex Haley was one of the few Black people who were able to trace his ancestry to Africa but how many Black people have not been able to do that? By studying about African Americans, people can try to change for the future and educate more people, especially young Black students. Schools do not give them enough information about slavery and the reconstruction period. I have learned a lot of things about Black people ever since I have taken African American courses at Berkeley High School. I was told Berkeley High was the only high school in the nation with an African American Studies Department. Since then I was more curious about the history of my people, and I wanted to learn more so I can educate my children and others.

I could go on about how much African American Studies is needed in schools, but I had to show the significance of the culture and literature in the life of African Americans. The literature, arts and history can tell you almost everything about Black people and their social issues. That is why having an African American Studies Department is an important part of education and life.

Joy Sledge
AAS 100
3-2-03

THE ROLES OF AFRICAN AMERICAN WOMEN

In the mid- 1800's to the early 1900's, African American women were seen as the jezebel or the mammy. As times and the tasks changed, Black women were seen as intimidating and still a jezebel. In *Soul Food*, the series, Terri (the sister who was a lawyer) intimidated her colleagues at her firm. She was the one of the best they had, but because she was an African American female, they would not make her partner. If she was a Black man, they might have made her partner since there were men in the partnership. Since she was a female, she would be the only woman and Black person in their partnership. Then when you saw music videos, Black women were "shaking [their] ass" (which is a song by a rapper named Mystikal), but you did not see White women doing the same thing. This is all related to how society sees Black women, but these images are not positive ones. If the woman is doing good, similar to Terri, she is still seen as bad because she intimidates people; they know she has the power to walk out. If she is a jezebel, she is seen as a whore and not good for society.

Ann Arnett Ferguson discussed in her book, *Bad Boys*, how the girls in sixth grade were taught by the teacher to act like a lady and not like a fool.

> "African American boys and girls who misbehaved were not just breaking a rule out of high spirits and needing to be chastised for the act, but were adultified, gendered figures whose futures were already inscribed and foreclosed within a racial order: Two girls, Adila and a friend, burst into the room followed by Miss Benton a black sixth grade teacher and a group of five African American boys from her class. Miss Benton is yelling at

the girls because they have been jumping in the hallway and one has knocked down part of a display on the bulletin board. . . This is what she says: "You're doing exactly what *they* (Italics are added) want you to do. You're playing into their hands. Look at me! Next year they're going to be tracking you."

One of the girls asks her rather sullenly who "they" is.

Miss Benton is furious. "Society, that's who. You should be leading the class, not fooling around jumping around in the hallway. Someone has to give pride to the community. All the black men are on drugs, or in jail, or killing each other. Someone has got to hold it together. And the women have to do it. And you're jumping up and down in the hallway."

. . . The teacher's words to the girls are supposed to inspire them to leadership. The message for the boys is a dispiriting one." (84-85).

Ferguson pointed out how the teacher taught the girls that they had a responsibility to the African American community; they needed to keep it strong and together otherwise it would collapse. The teacher was teaching the girls to stand up, act mature because they would not be taken seriously if they work in a professional field. When the girl asked who is "they," that showed she was not taught about society and how they viewed Black people.

Black women and girls have to be taught how to act and how not to act in a public place. Their public behavior makes people stereotype them. Everyone has stereotypes, but African Americans need positive stereotypes, not negatives. Also, the way the teacher spoke to them was a way of showing she cared. A White teacher would not have taught them how to act, and the teacher would have sent the girls to the Punishing Room (a detention room in the book where misbehaving students went, mainly Blacks).

This reminded me of when I was growing up going to a public elementary school. Boys would grab on my body parts and pretend everything was okay. When I told my mom what happened, she taught me it was not right, and when someone did something against my wishes, it had to be reported. My mom said, "Are you sure they touch your breasts because if you are lying that will make us look bad." I told her I was honest, and I reported the misbehavior to the principal. It was the way she said "You will make us look bad" that caught my attention, and I was only in the second grade.

I always wondered what she meant by "*us*," but as I got older I understood more, Black women and personally, me (people would not be able to trust me). I was taught not to be passive about sexual acts that boys did to me. If I did not like it I must stand up. I have self-respect, and society views Black women with no self-respect and promiscuous. This was another reason why the White lawyers at Terri's job would not make her partner, because of her "mouth."

Black women have big mouths that get them in trouble; they are seen as the "angry Black woman." When Black women are taught to speak up and speak their minds, White people do not like it. They fear something bad will happen, and Black people will start a riot. I have a cousin who will not kiss people's butts; however, since she knows she should be promoted she learned she has to kiss a little butt to get somewhere otherwise she will never be promoted because of her mouth. This is one of the problems Black women face in the professional world. Black men do not have the same problems as the women and there is no better or worse treatment for the women compared to the men because they are equal, it is just the gender that defines how they should be treated.

African Americans, particularly women, are taught to stand up and fight for what is right, but it is hard to do that if it involves their job. The professional world already has negative perspectives on African Americans, and we do not want to encourage that thought, but we want to change it. As a Black woman, I know when I leave college and become a lawyer or whatever I want to be, I know I have to make sure I carry myself the right way, without making people feel intimidated. In my sign language class, there are three other students who teach with me and all four of us sign a little different. One of the girls (she is Korean) who teach with me felt I was upset with her because I was telling her the correct way to sign. I told her I was not mad at her, but it was frustrating for the students to see two different signs. I hardly knew the girl, and she already felt I was mad at her. I believe it was because of the stereotype of Black women. I see for a Black woman to make it seem as if everything is all right, she has to act like a "sambo" for people not to feel intimidated by her, and it is wrong. We do not want to have the stereotype of being the jezebel or passive; it is hard to define our roles as Black women. I know it is up to us to demonstrate that not all of us fit the negative roles but to show that we are capable of leading and living seriously.

Joy Sledge
AAS 100
4-21-03

THE NEGATIVE REPRESENTATIONS OF BLACKS ON TELEVISION

African Americans cannot be represented in one film but in many. It is hard to use one film as a representation because there are different films that represent Blacks in different ways. There are a few good movies about African Americans, but many negative images of Blacks since D.W. Griffith's *Birth of a Nation*. *Birth of a Nation* has set the trends of negative perspectives on Blacks and that perspective is still here now. Black women played roles as mammies or jezebels (*Imitation of Life* and *Carmen Jones*). The Black men were Uncle Toms (*Uncle Tom's Cabin*) or oversexed since they wanted the pure White women. These roles are seen today in Spike Lee's *Jungle Fever* and various other movies. The few good movies of Blacks are *Lean On Me* (but the principal, Joe Clark was called "Crazy Joe" because he exercised his power to shape up his school), *Soul Food* (the series is better than the movie since you get a sense of what happened outside of family matters), and *Stormy Weather*. In these movies, Blacks played respectable roles; they were not seen as buffoons and clowns.

The majority of Black movies are silly and stupid. I asked myself, "Why is this movie out?" The stupid and ridiculous *How High*, with rappers Method Man and Redman was awful and in the film, they attended Harvard University. Method Man received an "A" in his chemistry class because he created a "weed" serum to get people high. What is so intelligent about that? Then two pimps were asked to teach a class called "Pimpology I and II." They taught their students how to smack their "ho's" and "dog" females. Again, this was at a respectable university, and these Black men were not taking their education seriously nor did the dean.

In fact, the dean found ways to get them expelled from the school, but instead the dean got fired and the guys were able to stay. Many young Black people saw this movie and enjoyed it since that was their take on what college would be like. College was not anything like this and these two rappers made fun of how school should be. One of the greatest college movies I enjoyed was John Singleton's *Higher Learning*, with rappers Ice Cube, Busta Rhymes, and actor Omar Epps.

Ice Cube taught Epps about Black history and how White people owned everything in America. These young educated Black men got into a fight with a White supremacy group and the Blacks won the fight. However, when Ice Cube said they still lost and Epps asked how, Cube said, "Look around you. White people own this country, this school, this couch we are sitting on, the clothes on your back and YOU." That line made me think, and I was only twelve years old when I saw this movie. Ice Cube showed an intelligent, educated mind, and it was great to see two rappers at Colombia University dealing with real life issues. Higher Leaning was the type of movie young Black people needed to see with Black people in college. Not a movie where Blacks go create a weed serum and turn the university upside down.

What about *Undercover Brother* and other countless stupid Black movies? Now I can look at the title and the actions and say, "I do not want to see it." The last Black movie I saw in the theatre was *Drum Line*, which was about a Black college competing in a drum competition with other Black colleges. The movie was good and there was not any nudity or a lot of profanity. It was said Denzel Washington's *Antwon Fisher* (based on a true story) was a respectable film, but not a lot of Blacks saw it. Washington, who won an Oscar earlier that year, was a respectable actor/director and not enough Blacks saw his film. However, they were willing to see him in *Training Day*, where he played a corrupt cop. During the time when *Antwon Fisher* came out, *Friday After Next* came out and many Black people saw it. I do not feel Black people get the credit they deserve when they play roles that are not drug dealers, crack addicts and other roles that always make Blacks look bad. When people of other races see these films, they assume all Blacks are like this because there are so many movies about us in the 'hood, in jail, athletes and etc. People do not see the intelligent roles we play as lawyers, teachers and business owners.

As I have said before, I can go on about the different shows and movies that do not represent African Americans in a positive way.

The Parkers, on UPN, showed a single mother raising a sort of dumb daughter, and they went to a junior college together. I gave credit to the mother because she was trying to get her life back together, but the daughter was ignorant who did not seem to know the basic things in life. The way they were portrayed embarrassed me as a Black female because she was making some Blacks look bad in terms of how much she knew. Also, the mother embarrassed me because she chased her professor and tried to convince him to be her boyfriend. She did not form a bond with him but stalked him and got into his apartment. She was supposed to be the independent woman trying to get her life together, instead she was showing she was desperate for a man. Her actions showed even though she looked like a mammy (her size), she was a jezebel in a way because she continued to harass her professor. Two other shows where they have at least one dumb child in the family were *The Hughleys* and *My Wife and Kids*. You would think they would have sense and knowledge, but the dumb skit in comedies are not funny anymore. I do not know if it is television or me, but Black shows need to improve and move on. As Womack said in *Bamboozled*, "It's the same shit, just done over, and I'm rising above it" (the words may not be exact but that was his point).

Joy Sledge
AAS 100
5-5-03

BLACK LEADERS AND WHERE ARE THEY?

The problem with the African American community or life is we do not have any leaders. If we had leaders, maybe we would be a lot better and more active. The reason why we do not have any leaders is because of the Federal Bureau of Investigation (FBI) and Counter-intelligence Program (COINTELPRO) instigations and infiltrations. Malcolm X, Martin Luther King, Jr. (MLK), Black Panther Party (BPP) and others have been assassinated or destroyed because the FBI felt threatened by them.

They did not want any Black people trying to uplift their people, and they did not want any Blacks to be anti-White/ "cop killers." No one feel as if they are able to stand up for what is right. They are afraid of being killed or incarcerated such as some of the members in the BPP. FBI and COINTELPRO have been targeting against Blacks and their activities since the early 1900s; they still target us to this day.

J. Edgar Hoover had been associated with the FBI since 1919 until 1972. Whenever one heard his name, some people knew what it meant. In *Racial Matters*, by Kenneth O'Reilly, he discussed the origin of the FBI and COINTELPRO and how they had been used to bring down Black activists.

> "The history of the Federal Bureau of Investigation and the history of black American have been linked together almost from the Bureau's beginning in 1908, when Charles J. Bonaparte . . . established a "Bureau of Investigation". (The word "Federal" was added in 1935). The Bureau's decision to avoid protecting civil rights and to spy on blacks were more in reaction to directives from the White House and the Justice Department than results of its own policy. In 1910, during the second year of William Howard Taft's presidency and in response

to a series of particularly brutal lynchings, the Department claimed "no authority . . . to protect citizens of African descent in the enjoyment of civil rights generally". Expected by the Wilson's administration to confine itself to gathering political intelligence on the "Negro Question," the Bureau paid little attention to day-to-day violations of federal civil rights laws- let alone to the episodic blood rites committed by the Ku Klux Klansmen and other white supremacists to enforce deference and submission" (9).

This statement justified why the FBI was created and who they were working for. They were supportive of the KKK, and they did not want any Black people to rebel and uplift their people. COINTELPRO was not started until later in the mid-1900s. "The FBI launched a new counterintelligence program, patterned after the Communist party and Ku Klux Klan operations, that targeted civil rights movement leaders and black power advocates alike under "Black Hate Group" caption" (261, O'Reilly).

This showed how much surveillance the government had over Black leaders and activists. COINTELPRO was a branch from the FBI to focus more on the black activists, while the FBI could focus on other things going on in the Black or other communities (Chicano and other "minorities"; minorities is quoted because really people of color are the majority). Since these organizations from the FBI had so much power and hate, that was how they infiltrated and destroyed many of the civil rights movement and black power movement.

Malcolm X was part of the Nation of Islam (NOI) since the early 1950s, when he was released from prison. While he was a minister for NOI, the FBI never targeted him because he never spoke about politics. However, in a sense he was targeted later because NOI was seen as a Black hate group or anti-White. All Malcolm X expressed was why Blacks should uplift themselves instead of depending on the "White man" and how the "White man" brainwashed them.

FBI infiltrated the NOI by spreading rumors about Elijah Muhammad and his affairs. Muhammad thought Malcolm had spread the rumors about him and banned him from NOI. While Malcolm was banned, he went to Mecca and learned about the real religion of Islam.

He learned blonde-hair, blue eyed Muslims were welcomed with the brown skinned Muslims. When he came back to America, the FBI targeted him because he changed and started believing in what MLK said about races integrating. Muhammad hired some gunmen to kill Malcolm.

He was afraid of Malcolm spreading the word of the real Islam and how the NOI was not as real as it was in Africa and the Middle East. The FBI divided these two men and conquered because one of the greatest Black leaders was murdered. MLK was threatened to quit his leadership or have his family affairs become known to the public. The FBI tapped into his phone and put a "bug" in his house to tape record what happened between him and his wife. Three years after Malcolm X's death, MLK was assassinated. Two of the greatest Black leaders were gone in the 1960s simply because they were trying to help their people rise up and stand up for themselves. Although MLK and Malcolm were against each other, in the end they came together to help their people. The government felt threatened by the two men. They were educated and they were not "dumb" and in order to get rid of them, they had to be "gone."

As for the BPP, FBI and COINTELPRO were watching them closely since these were armed Black people who were also intelligent. In *Liberation, Imagination, and the Black Panther Party*, Kathleen Cleaver and George Katsiaficas discussed how the FBI had been targeting the BPP since it was first organized.

> From the very earliest days of party organizing efforts, the FBI surveilled BPP activists and sent copies of their reports to other agencies of government, including Military Intelligence (MI), Naval Intelligence (NISO), and the Secret Services, among others, under the rubric RM-"Racial Matters" (48).

Huey Newton and Bobby Seale were in college when they were participating in Black organizations in Oakland, California. However, Newton was in law school studying people's rights to bear arms for protection and reading the laws to help inform other Blacks of their rights. When they were watching a cop beat some Black person, the BPP were armed to let the police know if they hurt them, they had the right to protect themselves.

The police felt threatened because the BPP were dehumanizing them, calling them "pigs" to show them how it felt when the Whites were calling Blacks "monkeys." As more BPP chapters opened all over the US, FBI had to find a way to tear them apart, and one of them was the newspaper. "The BPP newspaper has a circulation in excess of 139,000. It is the voice of the BPP, and *if it could be effectively hindered it would result in helping cripple the BPP*" (emphasis added) (48, Cleaver and Katsiaficas). As more and more BPP leaders/ members were either arrested or murdered, the BPP chapters were turning against each other. Eldridge Cleaver and Huey Newton were against each other, and they were on two separate coasts (Huey, west and Cleaver, east). The FBI had divided them and conquered the BPP because members were dropping out and going to other organizations (NOI, Black Liberation Army [BLA], and etc.). The FBI was mailing letters to Newton and Cleaver, signed by either of them turning them against each other. They infiltrated the BPP by also having "planted" Black people go to the meetings and reporting back to them. The BPP only existed for six years, from 1966-1972, and it was gone in 1972 because people wanted to take over and ignore the other chapters. The FBI and COINTELPRO was a success in bringing down the Black Power Movement and its leaders.

Today we do not have any leaders because within a two-decade period, Black leaders were assassinated or incarcerated. These were intelligent Black people, and the government felt threatened by them. These people were not going to keep being oppressed. As more and more Black organizations were forming, the government was doing everything it could to keep them under their thumbs. "The first thing the enemy tries to do is isolate revolutionaries from the masses of people, making us horrible and hideous monsters so that our people will hate us" (181, *Assata*). Assata was a member of the BPP and the "mother" of the BLA. The FBI and COINTELPRO were always watching her because of her involvement in the BPP. After the FBI posted "wanted posters" of her, she went underground until she was arrested for "killing a cop" and imprisoned for over 5 years. As Assata Shakur stated in her autobiography:

> "I do not think it's just an accident that we are on trial here. This case is just another example of what has been going on in this country. Throughout Amerika's history,

people have been imprisoned because of their political beliefs and charged with criminal acts in order to justify that imprisonment" (167).

What she said was true, which explains why many Black leaders were disappearing around the time she went underground. She knew the FBI was watching her because they tapped her phone and was the reason she went underground. While she was in jail, many people such as Angela Davis and others tried to have her freed. She was finally freed after over 5 years and when she was freed, she went to Cuba to hide out there. She demonstrated what her life was like as a BPP member and how COINTELPRO was always following her. She was one of the few to talk about her experiences, and her experience was very intense and scary because she had to change where she stayed every day.

Since the 1970s, the latest thing that happened with the FBI and the Blacks was the east/ west coast rap scene between Notorious BIG and Tupac Shakur. Tupac was always a threat since he became a rapper and especially since his mother was a member of the BPP. He was a product of the BPP, and he was educated. He had a rap that said to kill a cop because a cop is going to kill you. Afterwards, the government targeted him; he was a threat. Shakur was about survival in the ghetto because he knew what it was like to grow up without a high school education and rapping/ hustling were his ways of surviving. Then when it came to Shakur and Smalls (Notorious BIG) rap feud, the FBI used it as a way for them to keep fighting.

The FBI instigated their feud and made it seem like either of them were out to kill each other, which was how two rappers were killed (most believe Shakur is not dead since he still had albums coming out to this day. Shakur predicted he would be killed so most Blacks believe he is hiding out somewhere). Smalls' mother and friend stated (*Biggie and Tupac* video) they knew the FBI was watching Smalls because they were taking pictures of the family and friends in the house. The night Smalls was shot, the police were nowhere to be found, which could be the FBI had planned his murder. Many Blacks to this day feel the FBI instigated the feud and because of that, these two rappers were gone. Even though they were not leaders, since they were rapping about hustling and pimping, they were icons. This showed how if a person was not a leader but a major icon within the Black community, the government was always going to put someone against someone else, similar to Cleaver vs. Huey, Malcolm vs. King, and etc. There has always been someone to compare to in the Black community when "all eyes are on them," which was how a feud started. As one rapper said, "I'm not willing to die for rap. I just want to make music." Many Blacks feel the same way about the community, they are not trying to die to uplift their people, but they are willing to help their community discreetly without it becoming a "nationwide" thing.

If we had leaders today, Black children and adults would have a lot more respect for themselves and their community. Some of the children do not know who Malcolm X is, but they are familiar with MLK since there is a holiday named after him. Many also do not know about the BPP and other Black organizations that tried to help their Black community. If only the government was not racist and conservative, then we would not have the problems we have today. We would not have lost our Black leaders because they intimidated the government.

This is one of the main problems we have today. Since the BPP collapsed, we have gone forward for a brief time, but we went back for a long time. Black schools are dilapidated, poor and the basic skills for Blacks have decreased and will continue to decrease until someone takes a stand to say that is not okay. People are afraid to stand up because they are afraid they would be imprisoned or worse and that fear needs to end soon (such as, no Black person is willing to be the first to run for presidency for the U.S., except for Reverend Jackson and Sharpton, because they feel they will be assassinated the first day they announce who is running for presidency; joking a bit but serious at the same time). Otherwise, the Black community is going to collapse and everything is going to be back to how it was during the 1950s. Why do we have to wait until a Black person was done wrong, like the Rodney King beating, to protest or riot when they should do it for the wrongs that are being done in the community? We should not, but we feel as if we cannot stand because we know we are going to be pushed down and we need to stop being passive about what is happening to us.

Joy Sledge
Soc 111
6-14-03

CLASS AND HOW IT AFFECTS THE FAMILY

Class status has a huge effect on family life. The lower the class, the higher the stress level is based on financial burdens. An "institutional" sociologist would explain when you are middle class or above, your financial problems will not be as bad. You can afford the necessities and have more opportunities. In *Lives on the Line*, Martha Shirk, Neil Bennett, and J. Lawrence Aber, discussed the different families who lived below or near the poverty line and how their lives were affected by the fact they did not make enough money to raise themselves above poverty. Most of the families had a high school education/ GED or no high school education at all. A few of the families expressed how they came from a family where education was highly valued, but they chose not to listen to their parents. They tried to make up for the mistakes they made by looking at what their family valued and trying to improve their circumstances. Educational levels have a huge impact on class; the higher your education, the more jobs you can receive and higher pay. Also, when you have a higher education you have more control over your work schedule and can raise your family without so much economic tension.

Although it was hard for me to pick a few people from the book to demonstrate the influences of class background, educational choices, and family support, I picked a couple of people by their race to show how even though they were of different races, their lives were similar to other people who were in poverty. I picked Ron and Megan; they were a couple and even though they were together, they struggled every day. Their lives were complicated when it came to the financial burdens they had.

> "Although marriage to Ron would elevate Megan and
> the three children above the poverty line because he earns
> a good income, the fact is that the family would actually

be worse off financially than it is now. With a combined income of $36,509, Megan and Ron would be making too much to qualify for the child-care subsidies that Megan now receives on the basis of her income alone. The catch is that the couple wouldn't be earning enough to able to afford child care for the three children" (11).

Megan got pregnant when she was a teen, and she quit high school. Ron also dropped out of high school, which was why they found themselves in tough situations. She always did well in school, but when she was in high school, she started doing poorly. "My mom was hurt big time when I dropped out, but I didn't care'... Megan's mother and stepfather were even more upset when she moved in with her boyfriend, Todd..." (12). She expressed how her parents felt about her dropping out, and she was showing how they supported her with her education. As she said when she was older, "I was eighteen and dumb. Nobody could tell me anything" (12), showed how she regretted not listening to her parents, and how she had to live with the circumstances of not getting a high school diploma. Without a high school diploma, a person's job choices are very limited. Sometimes they have to work two jobs to earn more money for the family and the bills. For Megan, she was paid $6.20 an hour for being a nurse at a nursing home, and her schedule was very tight since she was a mother of three children. If she had one child, she would have managed her income, and she would have been middle class. However, the environment she was raised in was poor, and when people are not exposed to other ways of life, they are bound to repeat the pattern of the community. Also, she could not afford to make more money; otherwise, she would lose her children's medical benefits and not be able to afford their medical treatment. She was caught in a catch-22 situation, and that is what happens when you give up on yourself and find yourself in a tough situation. The Lyles family found ways to get through the hard times and became a little more successful than Megan and Ron.

Celeste Lyles and her children seemed to make ends meet in order for them to do quite well for a family in poverty. Celeste managed to make her living arrangements better by working hard and finding support from her kin or friends. Celeste's mother had her at a young age, and Celeste had her first child when she was thirteen years old.

Later on when she had another child by another man, she dropped out of high school during her junior year. She said, "It was the worst mistake of my life" (206).

She had four children and some of her children were doing well in school, even though some may have had children of their own they still continued to go to school. One of her daughters went to college while she had a child to take care of and the younger daughter was doing well in school, too. She supported her children's educational goals. One of the ways she did it was by taking care of her grandchildren, while their parents worked or attended school.

As Black people, they had to learn how to adapt to their conditions because that was what Black people had been doing since slavery. The mother made sure her children received their education, and they attended church regularly to receive support from the community and from religion. Celeste and her friend have helped each other through hard times, which was how they managed to do well. Also, when Celeste did not have anyone to watch her younger children, she had her oldest son watch them. It was cheaper, and it was the only choice she had. Her son, Curtis said, "At the time it wasn't much fun. But I think it made me a better person. That's why I'm working and going to school. I want better in life for my kids" (209). He was happy his mother taught him responsibility because it made him realize if he wanted anything, he had to work for it. She gave them options of how to live, and most of them chose the successful route. They saw how hard it was for her as a single mother with four children.

Based on Celeste's model of living and giving a positive lifestyle for her children, my mother did the same for me. Although my mother was raised in a near middle class home, she was taught that education was the key of living a successful life. My grandfather went to college and served in World War II in order for him to live a "middle class" life. He put all of his children and grandchildren through college. Although my mother dropped out of college, she went to trade school (cosmetology and barber school) to earn a living for herself. She had me when she was twenty-four years old, which was a big difference from having me at sixteen years old. She had one child, and it was easier for her to take care of two people, rather than three or four.

She had options of birth control to make sure she did not have more children (women in poverty cannot afford birth control, which is how they have more children than intended). Her educational level made a difference in our lives. We are "middle class", and she told me one time "I was doing better than the other students in my class who had two parents." My mother made the right choices because she was exposed to the bigger world; her father had his college degree and her mother was willing to work. They showed her how to make positive choices and made sure she could support herself and her family. The life lessons she was shown were taught to me. She wanted to make sure I lived a positive life and could do things for myself.

The class background of people's families can make a difference in how they live their lives and raise their families. Meg and Ron, who were both high school dropouts, were struggling to get by and decide whether they should marry or not. The negatives outweighed the positives, and they found themselves in tough situations when it came to taking care of their children.

However, they were finally able to get married, and they bought a house, which emphasized how hard they worked to make sure they could improve their living conditions. Celeste had to teach her family the value of hard work to show there was a better way of getting the things she wanted, without giving up on herself. She did not want her children to repeat the cycle she went through and even though she was a grandmother, her children were still going to school trying to get their diplomas and degrees. Since her job was seasonal, she did not make as much money to support her family and buy them Christmas presents.

Her daughters were still doing well, while her sons were not, which showed the perseverance the family had. My mother was from a "middle class" background, and she was shown there was a path to college where she could live a better life and raise a child in a positive environment. Sociology revolves on how the larger circumstances around one influence who one is. These circumstances also influence the choices one make, which could be either good or bad. Also, it affects how you raise your family because your class status will either give you more options or limit your options.

Joy Sledge
ES N144
5-25-04

RESPONSE PAPER #1

Racial Formations in the United States, by Michael Omi and Howard Winant, discussed what is race and how it is different from the term racism. Race was constructed by the dominant society, particularly White people, to classify a group of people by their phenotypes, such as skin color, hair textures and etc. Race was used to determine who was superior to whom and make sure there was a social hierarchy in America's society. If a White person had children with a person of color, then they were seen as eliminating the "pure" white race.

> "Count Joseph Arthur de Gobineau] not only greatly influenced the racial thinking of the period, but his themes would be echoed in the racist ideologies of the next one hundred years: beliefs that superior races produced superior cultures and that racial intermixtures resulted in the degradation of the superior stock" (Omi and Winant, 64).

If more White people continue to have interracial relationships, then it means they will become the minority, and they do not want that. An example of this is the case where a White woman was 1/32nd black, and once a person had Black blood in them, they were considered Black. It did not matter if they looked White, if they had the "one-drop" of Black blood, they were considered Black. Even though the woman tried appealing her case to change her race to White, the court would not do it. She did not want to be seen as the oppressed people because by labeling her as "Negro" and not as the superior race, her self-esteem was lowered. The sad thing about this racial hierarchy in the White community was that it affected the people of color in their community.

In each racial group, they may have been against each other because of certain features they may have had or their skin color or their class status. People within a certain community began to label each other to make themselves feel superior to the people they think did not deserve their respect. For example, in the Latino and Black community, the light skinned were usually seen as the superior ones while the dark skinned were seen as inferior. This was traced back into slavery, and the Treaty of Guadalupe-Hidalgo, when the White community would favor the light skinned people over the dark skinned. That led to resentment and animosity in the community because people felt oppressed by their own people.

There was reason to believe White people favored the light skinned. They were seen as having White blood in them and they were becoming more similar to the White people. Instead of White blood eliminating the people of color race, it was helping them because having White in them meant they were closer to White people. They were moving up the social ladder. Light skinned Blacks were allowed to read or be educated while the dark skinned were not allowed to. It gave them certain advantages because of their phenotypes. It was interesting to see how racism from the dominant groups led to racism within people's community, putting them against each other. That is why it is hard for people of color to come together because of the racial hierarchy. It is easier for the dominant groups to conquer and control the oppressed people by dividing them.

Joy Sledge
ES N144
6-1-04

READING RESPONSE #2

Ian Lopez's *White By Law: The Legal Construction of Race* discussed various issues of how the law had set up race in America and who could "pass" and who could not. By pass, I mean how immigrants from different countries were able to become citizens and pass for White. If they were non-white then they were denied citizenship of America. Lopez stated, "Law influences what we look like, the meanings ascribed to our looks, and the material reality that confirms the meanings of our appearances" (113). In some of the other chapters that Lopez had written, there were examples of how the United States used the law to discriminate against someone because of their skin color or their appearances. One example of the United States discriminating against someone was a man named Bhagat Thind who came from India. He considered himself White because the Aryan race came to his country before Jesus was born. Therefore, he was "White" because he had many years of white blood in him. Because he looked similar to the Asians (or as The Court called him, an Asian Indian), they considered him non-white. Another incident was a Japanese man, Takao Ozawa, who tried to become a citizen because he considered himself "White." However, he was denied citizenship because he was Asian, despite the fact he lived in America for a long time.

These two cases are prime examples of the law constructing who were white and non-white. "The United States is ideologically a White country not by accident, but by design at least in part affected through naturalization and immigration laws" (Lopez, 117). Race was constructed to make sure White people controlled America, and the non-whites would have to obey the law. Inter-racial marriages were illegal. If people from different races had children, then it would be hard for the people in the judicial system to tell who were White and Black. They did not want to put a White person in jail or do anything to harm them. If they did it would mean their system was not working (Lopez, 117). There are white people who come in different shades, and if they are a little darker than the normal white complexion, then they are assumed to be a person of color. In fact, there are some white people who are darker than very light skinned black people. This demonstrates race is only "skin deep." Ozawa considered himself White because of his skin complexion, but because of his ethnicity he was not considered White. There is a difference between skin color and ethnicity. People come in all different complexions and from different parts of the world. If they do not fit into a specific category, then the American government has to create another label for them to make sure people know their place in society.

In addition to the marriages, it was a shame if a US citizen woman married an immigrant man outside of her race, she would lose her citizenship in America (Lopez, 128). This type of behavior reaffirmed the notion that the government wanted to make sure America continued to be predominately White, and they wanted to control people's private lives. This was related to what I said earlier about how the government did not want interracial relationships; they were afraid they would not be able to identify who was what race. They didn't and still do care about how we were no different from each, despite our skin color (*Race: The Power of an Illusion*). They wanted to be sure that if they were going to control people then they would do it based on people's appearances; it would be easier to track them down. Race is a system that is constructed to target people and make them feel inferior. To make sure this country would continue to be run by White men, they had to create a system to make sure they would always be in power, no matter what the circumstances may be.

Joy Sledge
ES N144
6-8-04

READING RESPONSE #3

No Equal Justice, by David Cole, explained the difference between being a person of color, particularly black people and being white in the legal system and how the law works in favor for white people. One particular statement Cole made was that "...We have established two systems of criminal justice: one for the privileged and another for the less privileged. Some of the distinctions are based on race, others on class, but in no true sense can it be said that all are equal before the criminal law" (9). This statement was the thesis for most of the readings because most of the readings have stated people of color have to abide by different laws than whites. Although the laws are the same, they change according to a person's color. For example, when Cole said on page 134, "Accordingly, even though black cocaine offenders in the federal system serve sentences on average five years longer than white cocaine offenders, the courts see no constitutional problem" (143). This emphasized the discrepancy of the legal system and how it worked differently in terms of a person's race and class. The fact that people of color went to jail for a cheaper version of another drug showed no matter how little the act was, they would still get in trouble for it. The fact that a black person stole a slice of pizza equaled one strike, but a white kid shooting up a school meant they would go to rehabilitation. They were not likely to commit serious crimes as a black person. This shows there is no equal justice for a person of color, because the laws are made to target them and put them in prisons.

In addition to all of this discrepancy, a person of color "had" to consent to police search because if they said no, when they had the right to say no, the police would search their things anyway. The police would not search a white person if they said no because they would assume they knew their rights; they have a private attorney if the police searched them without a warrant. However, not many people of color knew their rights and if they did, their rights were violated. They were considered not to have any rights when the police were around. For example, when a black person rode the bus and the police searched his things, he tried to appeal based on not being read his rights. If he said no, they would have searched his things anyway (Cole). The judge disregarded his statement because the police officer said they asked, and he "consented." It is hard to say no when you know if you defy their power, something worse could happen to you, such as being beaten or possibly killed. There were other articles that reaffirmed this type of behavior but Cole really explained how the law worked for people of color and how their rights would always be violated, no matter if they knew them or not.

Joy Sledge
ES N144
6-10-04

LAWS THAT APPLIES TO PEOPLE OF COLOR AND WHITES

"You have to be White to be prosecuted under white law, but you do not have to be Black to be prosecuted under black law" (Gilmore, 22) is an accurate statement for how the legal system works in America. In *You Have Dislodged a Boulder: Mothers and Prisoners in the Post Keynesian California Landscape*, Ruthie Gilmore discussed different issues women of color experienced while their children and family members were in prison. One of the problems Gilmore discussed was the "3 Strikes Law" because it targeted people of color, and they went to prison for petty crimes instead of crimes that were very serious. However, there were a small number of white people who went to jail under the "3 Strikes Law" because the system worked differently for them. This is one example of how the law works differently for white people and people of color. There are other examples, and this problem has been around since black people have been brought here from Africa. However, things are done differently now because racism is subtler than before; it is institutionalized.

The first time America distinguished the difference between white and black people was around the 1650s when two white indentured servants ran away with a black "servant." When these three men were captured, the court made it clear the white men were servants and the black man was a slave, which was the beginning of racial formation. From that day, black people were associated with slavery because it was the law. This was significant because it set the rules for different races, and it created racism in America. It made poor white people feel superior to people of color since they were no longer seen as their equal.

Racial formation was a new way of making sure anyone who was not white could not have the privileges white people had. As Michael

Omi and Howard Winant stated in *Racial Formation in the United States*, "In the U.S., the origins of racial division, and of racial signification and identity formation, lie in a system of rule which was extremely dictatorial" (67). America separated people according to race because they wanted to control people and people's lands. Also, they wanted control over people's lives, such as deciding if they should kill someone or snatch a person's child or family member since they were not seen as human or as a citizen. Racial formations was another form of white supremacy; it made people of color feel inferior and white people superior to them. This was all part of manifest destiny for the US government; it was about them taking over the New World and everything else that they think they could steal from people (a person's land, identity, family).

Since America had racial formations, they had to create laws (also known as racial prerequisites) to make sure people of color could not try to become white or pass as white. Some examples of this were the Bhagat Singh Thind and Takao Ozawa cases. Both tried to pass as white, but the court told them no. They were told they could not become citizens because they were non-whites. Thind thought he could pass as white because of his ancestry of Europeans coming to his country (India) and having white in his blood. The courts did not grant him citizenship because he looked like he was an "Asian-Indian" immigrant. Ozawa thought he could pass as white because he was white in color, and he lived and went to school in America. The court said he was "Oriental" so he could not get citizenship. These two men knew by passing as white, they would be able to have white privileges. They would have access to a variety of things blacks and Native Americans could not have access to.

Racial prerequisites made it harder for these men to become citizens and to have access to freedom in America. Whiteness became a property because of the privileges that white people were able to obtain. As Cheryl Harris said in *Whiteness as Property*, "The possessors of whiteness were granted the legal right to exclude others from the privileges inhering in whiteness; whiteness became an exclusive club whose membership was closely and grudgingly guarded" (283). If these two people could beat the system to get privileges, then the government would not be able to control them. The courts guarded who could be a "member" of the club because if more people passed as white, then it would mean that racial formations was not working and that anyone could get around the legal system that the government created.

By having whiteness as property, people of color began to see that as "us vs. them" since they were aware their skin color was being targeted. Due to the high number of lynching and killings that were occurring to people of color, they knew the law worked differently for them than for whites. However, if a person of color killed a white person, they would automatically die or go to court to get the death penalty. In *All the Brother Wanted Was a Ride: Lynching and Police Powers in Texas*, Larvester Gaither explained, "Between 1924 and 1972, 361 people were put to death in Texas; 70 percent of them were "nonwhite;" blacks constituted 63 percent of those killed" (200-201). Then he adds later, "If...the murderers of James T. Byrd are convicted and sentenced to death, it will be the first time in the history of Texas, and one of the few times in the history of the United States, that white offenders were sentenced to death for the murder of a black person" (201). This type of behavior demonstrated how the legal system worked differently for people of color and how the legal construction of race played a huge role in determining who got what type of sentencing. When Gaither said "nonwhites," that was a primary example that a person of color did not have to be black to be prosecuted under the black law. However, being white gave white people the privilege to get away with murder and continue hate crimes against nonwhites.

Another white privilege is the right to turn down police searches if they did not have a warrant for the search. The police did not target whites since they expected them to know the law, and if the police went against their will they would sue the police. However, the police manipulated the Fourth Amendment when it came to people of color because people of color knew they did not have a choice. Most people of color did not know they had the right to turn down searches, but if they did they knew the police would go against their will. In *No Equal Justice*, by David Cole, he stated, "...Those who are coerced into giving their consent are most likely to be the young, the poor, the uneducated, and the nonwhite" (28). This was racial profiling since people of color did not always know their rights. They either did not have the money to afford a lawyer or they might have not had anyone in the family who was a lawyer. Most white people had relatives or friends who were lawyers, so they were aware of their rights; they could have a lawyer present anytime they want. That was why the police did not usually target them since they knew they would get in trouble if the search was illegal. They targeted people of color because it was part of racial profiling, and they could abuse their power on people of color.

Committing crimes are perceived differently when it comes to white people and people of color. White people get more leeway, and they get smaller punishments than people of color. In fact, white people may not have to go to prison if the crime was not considered "serious." An example of this is drugs in the white community. Cocaine is very expensive, but if a white person is caught with cocaine they may get rehabilitation or jail with probation. However, crack is a cheaper form of cocaine, and if people of color are in possession of crack they get 15 years in prison. A person with a large amount of cocaine gets the same time as a person with a small amount of crack. As David Cole said about white people using marijuana, "In the 1960s, however, marijuana spread to the white middle and upper classes... The harsh penalties imposed when their effect was primarily felt by minorities were no longer acceptable, and marijuana laws were liberalized" (152). The laws changed when a person of color was no longer the one committing serious crimes because the system did not want to put many white people in prison. Instead, they "liberalized" the laws so whites could get away with things people of color could not get away with. "When the effects of a criminal law reach the sons and daughters of the white majority, our response is not to get tough, but rather to get lenient" (Cole, 153). This demonstrated that a person had to be white to get more freedom and privileges, and if they were a person of color they had to suffer the consequences. This is a huge double standard in our legal system because the law is supposed to be justice for all, but it is justice for people who are the privileged.

These four various examples have been demonstrated show how the law changes depending on a person's race or skin color. The law is supposed to mean the same thing for everyone, but in reality there is a system inside the laws to help people who have privileges, such as white people. People do not have to be black to be prosecuted under black law. Anyone who is not white cannot get the same resources white people get. People of color get awful public defenders while white people have their own private attorneys. People of color are always profiled racially while white people are not. Then worse of all, people of color go to prison for petty crimes while white people who commit serious crimes get less severe punishment. These things are happening in our country, and it has been around for a long time. People know these things are occurring, and it is no mystery why but our legal system has an effect on who gets away with punishment and who does not. Racism is not as blatant as it used to be, but it is still here because it is institutionalized in our minds. This institutionalized racism is in our legal system and it has a negative effect on people of color and a positive effect on whites.

Joy Sledge
ES N144
6-15-04

READING RESPONSE #4

The Intersection Of Race and Gender, by Kimberle Crenshaw, discussed the contradiction women of color face when they were victims of violence. Women were taught to stand up for their rights, and any type of violence against women should be reported. However, when something horrible happened to a woman of color, society blamed her for what happened, and her story was not seen as important as the violence against white women. "Race, gender, and other identity categories are most often treated in mainstream liberal discourse as vestiges of bias or domination-that is, as intrinsically negative frameworks in which social power works to exclude or marginalize those who are different" (Crenshaw, 357). It is hard to separate your skin color from your gender or your class because the first thing that people see is your skin color then the other social categories to consider if you are a valuable person or not. For example, in one incident there was a Latina who was abused by her husband, and she tried to contact the women's shelter. However, the shelter refused to help her because she could not speak enough English to participate in the group meetings. Middle-class white women operated the shelter, and they turned the Latina away because she was not worthy enough to be sheltered from her husband. Now the person who referred the Latina to this shelter was worried the woman could be dead or on the streets because someone refused to focus on the mission, which was to get women out of awful situations.

It was not just violence that society blamed the women of color for, but also the increase of crack babies or babies out of wedlock. For the babies born out of wedlock, society placed the blame on the women for not having any morals or not being responsible for their children. Birth control and abortion were perceived as good things for women of color while they were seen as bad things for middle-class white women. *Racism, Birth Control and Reproductive Rights* explained that laws had been passed to sterilize women of color after they had their baby without their consent (Angela Davis, 214). Society felt they had the right to control how many babies a woman of color could have because they felt she was a drain on the economy (welfare). A lot of these women did not know they were sterilized until they tried to have children again or a doctor told them. This was an intersection between races, gender and class because depending on a woman's color and class she was seen as irresponsible and not worthy to have children. The government made decisions on what to do to her body without her knowing and that was a violation of her rights.

In addition to the irresponsibility of women of color, black mothers were seen as child abusers for having crack in their system when they were pregnant or delivering a baby. Dorothy Roberts explained in *Killing the Black Body* how black women went to jail for child abuse and not for doing crack. Although they did go to jail for crack, they would not do as much time as for if they were pregnant or had children. She argued that white women smoked marijuana and did crank when they were pregnant, but they did not go to jail because they were middle class. However, the women who did crack were black and poor, so it would not matter because she was draining the government by being on welfare and using the government's money on drugs. Again, she was blamed for creating the "crack baby" while really the babies who suffered the most are babies whose mothers smoked cigarettes and drank alcohol. Although crack was dangerous for the baby, it did not cause as many health problems as the babies who were born with fetal alcohol syndrome and other problems. This demonstrated that depending on the woman's skin color, society will decide who should be blamed for the problems occurring in America and who should not. Also, they will agree that women of color asked to be raped, or they had the programs to get off drugs. In reality these women were in a world all by themselves because they either lacked or could not get support to fight their circumstances.

Joy Sledge
ES N144
6-22-04

READING RESPONSE #5

People have different views of affirmative action and whom it works in favor for. In *The End of Racism* by Dinesh D'Souza, it explained how white people thought affirmative action worked in favor for people of color.

> "Like discrimination of the old sort, it employs racial classification to prefer less qualified members of some groups over more qualified members of other groups. The new discrimination is legal, as the old used to be. What differentiates the new discrimination is that it targets white, especially white males, and sometimes Asians" (290-291).

White people felt affirmative action gave away their spots in schools and employment to the people of color. They felt it was reverse discrimination because they felt their privileges were not allowing them to get the things they wanted. Affirmative action works for different people, such as disabled athletes, and they do not really get mad at them for getting the spots. When it came to people of color they attacked them and said it was reverse discrimination. They thought it was a racial issue, and they were not qualified for the job.

In the video *Secrets of the SAT*, the video watched a couple of white students, two Mexicans, two Asians and one black student during the college application process. The white students received high SAT scores while the Mexican and Asian students received high scores too. The black student received a low score, but he still got into University California, Berkeley. While one white student was rejected from University California, Berkeley, he appealed and got into University California, Berkeley. Some of the other people of color did get in and some did not. The point is even though the black student did not score high on the SAT's he still got in because of his merit. However, the white student felt he should have gotten into University California, Berkeley because of his grades and SAT's. The other students of color did not appeal when they did not get in because they probably did not know they could. This demonstrated how some people felt they deserve to be there and how some felt lucky they got in. The black student got in without affirmative action, and that made him feel like he got in because of his background and the obstacles he overcame as a student and as a person, which is how people should be selected. If there was affirmative action, the white student would have said the black student got in because of the quota to fill the spot, not for how hard he worked.

However, affirmative action only works for a small number of people of color. Really the people who were getting the jobs and spots in schools were people who network with the people in power of these corporations. Charles R. Lawrence III and Mari J. Matsuda's *We Won't Go Back: Making the Case for Affirmative Action*, explained how people really got the things they wanted by giving money to the schools or knowing the people who were in charge of getting people the positions. "Along with the privilege brought by wealth and connections is the unconscious arrogance of such power, and perhaps the conscious design to ensure royal treatment" (96-97). This demonstrated if people had money and connections then they were guaranteed positions because they gave to get something in return. While the privileged people were complaining that people of color were taking their spots, they should have been complaining about how people who had wealth and good connections were really taking the spots. People do not want to challenge the wealthy because they know that the wealthy can make or break them, whereas it is easier to make people of color the scapegoats of the problem. It is ironic how affirmative action is seen as a bad thing since it is for minorities, when it is the networking that is really taking the positions since it is for the people who have wealth. Affirmative action can be good in some situations, but at the same time it is nice to know a person got hired because of merit and not for the color of their skin or their gender. The problem is the privileged feel they should be entitled to the things they always had, but now that the oppressed people are in the front of the line they do not like the treatment and the fact they are getting a taste of their own medicine.

Joy Sledge
ES N144
6-26-04

HEAVY POLICING ON WOMEN OF COLOR'S REPRODUCTIVE SYSTEMS

Women have always been perceived as unequal to men and they should be in the home and not the workforce. However, women of color have always been perceived as someone to police and oppress because of their status in America. The status of women of color intersects because they have to worry about their race, gender and class and how it affects their life in America. White women have to worry about their gender and class, but because they are white they are entitled to things women of color cannot access. They are not blamed for society's problems whereas women of color are. Women of color, particularly black women have been blamed for the disruptions in the family and for raising children under bad social conditions. Due to the fact they are seen as welfare queens and producing a crack addicted generation, they receive heavy policing for these types of behaviors. There are different forms of policing for each situation, but in some ways the policing are the same because the government is controlling the women of color's reproductive systems.

Rape is a traumatic thing to happen to any woman. However, if a white woman was raped, then society sympathized with her, and if a black woman (and woman of color) cried rape it was perceived as if she deserved it. Black women have always been seen as sexual beings and "impossible" to rape. In *The Intersection of Race and Gender*, Kimberle Crenshaw says,

> "Sexualized images of African-Americans go all the way back to European's first engagement with Africans... these sexualized images of race intersect with norms of women's sexuality, norms that are used to distinguish good women from bad, madonnas from whores. Thus,

black women are essentially prepackaged as bad women
in cultural narratives about good women who can be
raped and bad women cannot" (369).

This statement explained why black women were seen as bad
women because of the notions that have been passed down from generations. The black woman was seen as oversexed, and if she claimed
she was raped society would say it was her fault because she was the
"jezebel." The perceptions of the black woman's body were that it was
made for men to take advantage of, whereas the white women's bodies were seen as pure and virtuous. "If these sexual images form even
part of the cultural imagery of black women, then the very representation of a black female body at least suggests certain narratives that
may make black women's rape either less believable or less important"
(Crenshaw, 369).

The negative stereotypes of the black woman's body enforced the
notion that black women are not respectable in America's society and
that they have no morals. The stereotype is stuck with black women,
and it makes society see them as bad women who will be bad mothers, contributing too many problems in America. White middle/upper
class people see her as the reason why there are no fathers in the
household because she cannot "keep her legs closed," and she keeps
making babies to collect money from the government. It has a trickle-
down effect on black women's socioeconomic status and it makes sure
that they are at the bottom of the social ladder and makes it harder for
them to climb up.

Since black women are blamed for putting themselves in situation
to be raped, they are also blamed for their social conditions and how
they live. They may not have a high school diploma or have the money
to go to college. Sometimes the women who do not have a high school
diploma are most likely going to become pregnant and since good pay-
ing jobs hire people with a high school diploma or a college degree,
these women may not be able to get the jobs. Without them having
good employment, they have no choice but to go on welfare to provide
for their children and themselves. However, by them being on welfare, they are seen as "welfare queens" because they are draining the
money from the rich people who pay taxes. The people who paid taxes
felt these women should get a job or put restrictions for them to have

welfare. One of the restrictions was the Learnfare program, where the caseworkers watch the teenagers whose parents were on welfare. The objectives of Learnfare were to:

> "Encourage teenagers in AFDC households to complete high school or its equivalent, thereby acquiring the minimum level of education to become "productive" citizens and to establish a relationship of mutual responsibility between the state and AFDC recipients" (Nathalie Augustin, 146).

Augustin explained in her article, *Learnfare and Black Motherhood*, how the point of Learnfare was to make the teenager improve their life and get the mother off of welfare. It was too late for the mother to make something of herself so her children had to improve their social conditions, so they would not follow the same path as their mother. However, the catch was the children could not miss school because if they did, then their family did not qualify for AFDC anymore. This was a form of policing because if the children missed too many days in school, then they could not get money to eat to function better at school. This would contribute to more social problems in the black community because the child might have to steal food or money to survive. It was a vicious cycle. The child may become pregnant or go to jail because they were doing things to help them survive. Society would blame their mother for contributing to these problems since she did not have a diploma or degree to get a job and take care of her family. They would blame her for being lazy and letting her children get away with contributing to the high crime rate in America. The mother was being policed for having children without some form of higher education, and if her children messed up in school then she would be punished by not having any money to take care of her family. She would be seen as not being fit to be a mother, which will lead to more women of color getting sterilized without their consent.

Before the discussion of sterilization, there was another issue that needed to be discussed that would also contribute to why society thinks women of color should be sterilized. People in America do drugs, but the ones who get the most severe punishment are black women who are pregnant since some of them do crack. When a black person is convicted for doing crack, they do more time than a white person doing cocaine. However, if a black woman is pregnant and she does crack, she is seen as giving birth to babies who will be addicted to crack and contributing to making the children more dangerous. It is bad enough black women are seen as welfare queens but to be pregnant and convicted for doing crack emphasizes that they are bad and selfish mothers. In *Killing the Black Body*, Dorothy Roberts explained, "The monstrous crack-smoking mother was added to the iconography of depraved Black maternity, alongside the matriarch and the welfare queen. Crack gave society one more reason to curb Black women's fertility" (157). Society dismissed the fact that there were a few programs to help women of color get off drugs since if a person of color asked for help, the doctor would report them to the police. If a white person wanted help, they could go to rehabilitation and not get in trouble with the law for doing drugs. The fact that when women of color asked for help and were denied their access to treatment, meant society wanted to keep women of color at the bottom of the social ladder. They were making it harder for her to do better and get herself together. It was another form of policing because these women went to jail for asking for help and for reproducing, not for doing drugs. As Roberts stated, "The prosecutions are better understood as a way of punishing Black women for having babies rather than as a way of protecting Black fetuses" (154). The black woman was not only going to prison for doing drugs, but for having children and draining the economy. White America thought it was best she was in prison so there would not be any more children, so she could not get on welfare. Welfare and pregnant women on crack work interchangeably in policing women of color on their reproductive systems. If the woman has too many children, she does not qualify for welfare. If she is pregnant and did crack, she goes to prison.

What was ironic was Roberts explained white women do drugs (smoke cigarettes and drink alcohol), and they were not reported to the police because they were middle class. They knew their doctor/ patient confidentiality whereas women of color did not. Doctors of white women did not test them for drugs because they knew the patients, and the patients were wealthy. When it was a black woman, they automatically tested her for drugs when she was pregnant, especially if she went to a clinic that helped low-income people.

Also, women who smoked cigarettes and drank alcohol caused more serious health problems to the fetus than women who smoked crack. It was just a matter of which drugs were legal (cigarettes and alcohol), which drugs were not, and who were most likely to do illegal drugs. This emphasized how the system worked for white women and women of color. In order to get away with some things, a person has to be white because if they are a person of color the police or anyone in power is going to target them and watch them closely. All of these problems black women or women of color experienced were blamed on them for not doing better and for becoming a menace to society. To make sure the people who paid taxes did not take care of welfare queens or "crack addicted" babies, the government found ways to police a woman's reproductive system and made sure she did not have any more children. Sterilization is one of the main surgeries that doctors perform on poor women of color to make sure that they do not "breed" anymore.

Sterilization is legal in some states, especially in the south where it is predominately people of color. Women can be sterilized without their consent and the only way they know they are sterilized is when they try to have children again or a doctor will tell them. "By 1932 the Eugenics Society could boast at least twenty-six states had passed compulsory sterilization laws and thousands of 'unfit' persons had already been surgically prevented from reproducing" (Angela Davis, 214). The doctors decided who were going to be sterilized, and the majority of women of color were unaware they were sterilized. As Davis mentioned in *Racism, Birth Control and Reproductive Rights*, it was not birth control but population control.

These women were seen as unfit mothers who "bred," and they were policed by not having control over their reproductive system. It was another form of slavery because they were severely punished while the baby was suffering. They did not have a mother, or because they belonged to the government. However, pregnant women of color who did drugs could prevent themselves from going to prison or prevent their children from getting caught in the system by agreeing to have an abortion or staying on birth control. Dorothy Roberts said, "When a pregnant woman is arrested for harming the fetus by smoking crack, her crime hinges on her decision to have a baby. She can avoid prosecution if she has an abortion... If she violates probation by becoming pregnant, she will be sent to prison" (152). This demonstrated how women of color were policed because of negative stereotypes about their bodies. They were seen as bad women and society felt they could punish bad women by making them incapable of reproducing. Black children who were born to "unfit" mothers fell into the government's trap by committing a crime, and going to jail where the government made money from their labor. All of this is a system of putting people of color in prison, so the government can get their money back and build more prisons so they can profit from more labors. The "welfare queens" and prosecution of pregnant women are all part of the government's plans to have control over the population of people of color. They can control how many children people of color can have or they can put them in prisons to keep them off the street and make money for the government.

The welfare reform and prosecution of pregnant women of color for doing crack/ drugs are all related to the government's plans to trap the women of color into their prison of control. These two things, including the way the women of color are seen as whores, are all part of policing women of colors' bodies and making sure they do not "breed" and cause more problems in America's society. The welfare reform is a way of policing how many children a woman can have while she is on welfare because if she exceeds the limit then she is unqualified for the money. Incarcerating pregnant women for using crack is not for saving the fetuses, but for putting more people of color in prisons. Then sterilization or birth control is used to keep women from having any more children because if they do then chances are they will go to jail (if they are convicted), or their children will go to jail because of their socioeconomic status. This is not about trying to help fix black people or people of color's socioeconomic status, but it's a way to target them for being poor and living in poor conditions. It is a way to make white (and some middle/ upper class people of color) taxpayers feel safe and make sure they are getting their money's worth in protection. It is no mystery why poor/ low-income women of color's reproductive rights are being taken away from them, but it is all part of the intersection of race, gender, and class. The men do not give birth to the babies, and majority of the birth control are designed for women so it would be hard to control the men's reproductive system. It is easier to target the women because the hospital can report them. Also, in people of color's community (particularly blacks and Latinos), there are more female-headed households, and that is how the problems of the intersection of race, class and gender come into play in terms of who does society want to police.

Joy Sledge
ES 147
6-15-04

READING RESPONSE #3

Nada Elia's *A Woman's Place is in the Struggle* demonstrated how she was a woman who was Lebanese struggling with Americans' perceptions of Muslims and Middle Eastern people. One of her main arguments was women should be fighting for their rights and different struggles that were occurring locally and nationally. She discussed how she became a political activist and how she contributed in different ways to help people.

One thing I found significant was when she said, "My mother, my three sisters, and I now made up the Elia household. I grew up surrounded by people who believed that because none of us had a penis, we were worthless" (118). I thought it was interesting how the community saw her family as helpless women because there was not a man in the house. It was as if they did not see them capable of living independently and were not capable of taking care of themselves. Her mother thought they were capable of living without a man in the house because she explained later how her mom told her how important an education was. By her mom not being able to get an education but believing that it would help her daughters meant she was defying her culture by saying a woman did not have to depend on a man. Her mother had a lot of courage to break the traditional roles of women to tell her daughters to become someone.

Thanks to her mother, Elia is a writer, journalist and activist because her mother encouraged her to step outside of the gender box and do something useful. That was why she said, "Whether it be at home, at school, in the office or on the battlefront, a woman's place is still in the struggle" (119) because a woman can contribute in many ways that do not have to be confined in the home. Her struggle is everywhere because a woman is just as capable as any man.

Joy Sledge
ES 147
6-26-04

THE CONTRADICTION OF THE GENDER ROLES IN THE HOUSEHOLD

Black women have always been in the labor force. They have worked outside of the home since slavery, and they still continue to this day. Sometimes when a woman works, she intimidates her husband or male partner because it means she is not dependent on him. Her independence makes him feel like he cannot provide or contribute to the household. At the same time, when a woman works, the husband does his best to help his wife around the house; their gender roles are interchangeable. In the movie, *Soul Food*, two sisters worked and their roles outside of the home affected their home life in different ways by the way the men behaved in the home. The husbands tried to help the women relax from a stressful day at work by taking care of business in what they think represented their manhood. The discussion of intimidation within the spouse's relationship contradicted with the interchangeable roles the husband and wife took on, depending on their class status. This was all related to the traditional gender roles of the man being the productive labor and the woman being the reproductive labor, except in the film's case, some of the gender roles had switched.

Women have always been the reproductive labor because their job was to give birth and raise their children to become productive or reproductive. Men have always been the productive labor because their bodies were not in jeopardy to reproduce. Capitalism has set up the gender roles by making men the breadwinners and women taking the money and spending it in the market to make her home life more pleasurable. In *Women and The New International Division of Labor*, the author stated:

> "Whereas capitalism as an overarching political economy defines class relations, patriarchy, a system subor-

dinating women to men on the basis of gender, defines gender relations. The primary locus of patriarchy is the household, where relations of production and reproduction are maintained through ideologies emphasizing male authority" (34).

By having women stay at home, they were becoming dependent on their husbands to provide for them and make the decisions for the household. Men made sure the women obeyed them and they were the authority figure. However, when the women worked, the women got to have a little authority because they were earning money, and they could control what was going on in their household. As the author stated on page 43, "Men's objection also reflects the threat that women's wide-scale employment may undercut the patriarchal status quo based on women's symbolic assignment to the domestic mode of production." Men did not like women making money because it took away their authority in the home. Also, the women's jobs took jobs away from men, and they felt as if there were not enough employments for them. "...Women's labor...weakens the family by eroding women's domesticity and impairing male breadwinners' wage-earning ability" (43). Men felt if the women work, then the family structure was weak because there was not a balance between the home and work force. With the women working, intimidated the men because the women demonstrated she did not need the man to be the provider, and she could take care of herself. This type of behavior is seen in all ethnicities, but in the American culture, this type of behavior is seen heavily in the working class through middle class African American community.

When Black women work, they demonstrate that they are independent and strong because they know they have to work to provide for their families. Gender roles were not the only thing capitalism constructed, but also the way people of color function in the work force, making sure men and women worked to provide for their families. It also has set up the notion of there is no such thing as gender roles in people of color community. In *Aberrations in Black*, Roderick Ferguson says,

> "The migrations of Asians, Europeans, Mexicans, and African Americans generated anxieties about how emerging racial formations were violating gender and

sexual norms. As racialized ethnic minorities became the producers of capitalist surplus value, the American political economy was transformed into an apparatus that implanted and multiplied intersecting racial, gender, and sexual perversions" (13).

Ferguson's statement demonstrated how capitalism functions in people of color's families and how capitalism changed the gender roles in the home. While the previous paragraph explained how men did not like women working, in the Black community, men had no choice but to accept their women working; they knew their income alone could not support the family. It was ironic how capitalism changed depending on a person's gender and race because if it was a White person, then capitalism was constructed by gender. If it was a person of color then capitalism was constructed by race and gender. In addition, White America thought it was weird how men and women were doing each other's work; it was something they did not do in their families. This demonstrated how different racial backgrounds have different views of what was women and men's work. In Black people's household, there were rarely gender roles because the community pitched in and everyone did each other's work. *Soul Food* portrayed how the woman could do the productive labor while the man could be getting back on his feet and how the man helped his wife around the home. However, the thing was one couple was still a little structured on traditional roles where the other changed their roles, depending on the situations.

In *Soul Food*, Bird was the youngest sister of the Joseph family and her husband, Lem had been convicted of a crime. Bird owned her business, which was a hair salon and Lem struggled to find employment. When Lem was fired, he went to Kenny, his brother-in-law for advice about how to get a job and how to tell Bird he did not have a job. Kenny looked at him with an expression that read, "You are stupid if you tell her, and she is going to kill you." With the expression on his face, he said,

> "No, no, you don't want to tell her, man... cuz you ain't got a job. No, you don't wanna tell a woman..." Then Lem adds, "A black woman." Kenny continues, "Especially a black woman that you ain't got a J-O-B. It's all right for

them to lie around the house, but let a man..." Lem adds, "A brother." Kenny continues, "Especially a brother..."

This demonstrated how a man felt when he did not have a job to support himself and his woman. Although Lem thought it would be best to tell Bird, he decided to keep it to himself because he did not want to worry her and cause tension in his home. This showed how he was taking care of business by asking for help and trying to be honest about the situation. Also, the part where Kenny said it was okay for women to "lay around the house," demonstrated how some gender roles are still prevalent in the Black community. This was similar to the quote from *Women and The New International Division of Labor* since Kenny felt the man should be running the home like a man should, whether the woman was working or not. Although the men were not upset about their women working, they were saying it was okay if she does not have a job, but it was not okay for them to be out of work. If a man is out of work then he feels like he is not a man because staying home is not considered masculine, and he could be seen as lazy. When Kenny emphasized the "Black woman," it showed how race and gender were affected by capitalism and when you add Black with woman, it did not sound good. He made it seem negative about not having work and being with a Black woman because of the cultural awareness a Black woman always works and if the men did not work, then she would complain about it.

When Bird found out that Lem was not working, she said, "Look, boo, the shop is doing really well right now, and there's a lot of people that comes through there. I'll see if anybody can hook you up with a job." Her statement angered Lem. He said, "Bird, I don't need your help! I can find my own damn job." If she helped him then he would not feel like a man. A man is supposed to find his own job and not feel like he is living off of his woman. Although she did not see her offer as a threat, he did. He wanted to contribute financially because if he did not, his self-esteem would lower, and he would not consider himself a man. This was all part of the traditional roles of men and women. Her statement intimidated him since he was raised that being a man meant doing everything for himself and his woman. If a woman provides everything, then the man will feel as if he does not have anything to offer. He has to make sure that he does his part while she does her part.

Teri, the oldest sister, was a lawyer as well as her husband, Miles. There was this scene where Teri arrived home from work and Miles was in the kitchen. He said,

> "I got your favorite tonight. Yeah, I spent hours slaving... Looks like that case is kicking your butt." Teri responds, "Yeah, I don't know how long the jury's gonna be out and the firm is really pushing me to be partner." Miles ask in a confused tone, "Well, that's what you want, right, to make partner?" Teri snaps, "Any attorney worth their salt wants to make partner."

This scene showed Miles as the sympathetic husband trying to help relieve his wife's stress. He was trying to make conversation about how work was going for her and was trying to let her know he cared. Teri had the attitude of a husband, who had a long day at work. Miles' role was similar to a wife's because he was trying to ask how Teri's day was and that he sympathized with what she was going through. This scene showed how their gender roles have switched and how the workforce made Miles help out around the home. He knew his wife was having a hard day, so he thought he could cook for her and make things easier for her in the home. His role as a husband contradicted Kenny and Lem's role as husbands since Miles was more modern and understood that a person marries someone who works extremely hard, they become partners with their spouse to keep a balance in the home and the workforce. Also, class has structured Miles behavior by how he got off work earlier than his wife, so he had the extra time to cook his wife a decent meal. Lem and Bird was middle class, and their lives were more traditional because Lem may have had to work longer hours than Bird, who could leave when she wanted since she owned her shop.

This movie showed the contradictions of gender roles and how class played a role in these contradictions. The Black family's gender roles are always changing depending on how the family feels about certain roles. The main idea is Black women are working and how does their work affect their husbands' role in the home. Who is more likely to take on some of the women's roles? Usually the working to lower class families have the idea that the men cannot just do house-work but must do the financial work. He has to help the woman finan-cially otherwise his manhood is threatened. The middle to upper class families understands their roles will change depending on how much money they make and how valuable they are at work. They know their home life revolves around their work life and the interchangeability of their gender roles does not threaten their gender. The subject of how does the man feel about the woman working is very contradic-tive and it is interesting to see how some men are intimidated if the woman is the breadwinner and those that are not intimidated, take on the women's roles.

DEAF STUDENTS AND SOCIAL FACTORS THAT AFFECT THEIR ACADEMIC PERFORMANCE (THESIS)

INTRODUCTION

As a child with a hearing loss growing up in Oakland, I had to face the injustices of the special education programs in public school systems since private schools tended not to accept children in special education. Oakland is a huge city. There are over 60 schools in the district, and the funds are not evenly allocated. Oakland public schools are majority African Americans, Latinos/ Chicanos, and Asian/ Asian Americans. The residents in Oakland are also mainly minorities (Bay Area Census). The "minorities" (how can people of color be minorities when we are the majority) go to Oakland public schools, while many whites go to magnet or private schools.

When I started school in pre-kindergarten, I was in a class with three or four other hearing "impaired" students (impaired is a derogatory term for hearing loss, but it is constantly used in the "hearing" society). The students were put together based on their hearing loss, meaning majority of my classmates were hard of hearing, whether their hearing was better or worse than mine. As the students got older, the teachers put the students together based on their level of class work. For example, when I was in the first grade, I was doing work of second or third graders. Some students learn faster than others, which is what an Individualized Education Program (IEP) is meant to allow in special education. Every year around a student's birthday, the teacher tested the students to find out what their strengths and weaknesses were. As Ernest Hairston and Linwood Smith discussed in their book, *Black and Deaf in America: Are We that Different*, "For each handicapped child there will be an "Individualized Educational Program" (IEP) that is a written statement of the child's educational goals developed by both parents and teachers" (27). The IEP is a legal document, which states what the students need in order to perform well in school. If the school does not provide the services, the parents can fight the district because the district is mandated to provide the services.

One of the things my IEP stated was I needed a Frequency Modulation (FM) system, which was a hearing aid that looked like a walkman, and the teacher had the microphone. With the FM system, I could only hear the teacher, even though there were background noises. However, my hearing aids picked up everything, including background noises, which made it harder for me to hear the teacher. I requested an FM system for two years and never once did I receive it while I was in Oakland. The school district was too poor to afford it even though a few of my classmates had one. A hearing aid alone, when I was younger cost about $500, which was $1,000 for a pair. Some of the students could not afford to wear two and when they finally got the second one, it was time for a new pair of hearing aids. I was fortunate to be able to have two hearing aids because they were expensive. The new kind that I am wearing now (the digital hearing aids) costs $1,000 for one, $2,000 for a pair. If hearing aids cost about $500 in the late 1980s, early 1990s, imagine how much the FM system would cost, possibly $2,000 or more. There was no justification to why the school could not provide my services when I had it written down in my IEP.

I had other needs as well, such as being mainstreamed with the hearing class and having speech therapy twice a week. Those were two of the few things that could be provided because one was free and the other was already there for the school. I had to be mainstreamed because I needed to interact with the hearing students, and I was capable of doing "regular" work. Thanks to being mainstreamed, I had the benefit of doing work that some of the other deaf students could not do. It helped boost my confidence in school, and I did not always feel excluded from the hearing students. Since I was usually mainstreamed, that was the main reason why I needed an FM system because my teacher could not sign American Sign Language (ASL). Also, I did not have an ASL interpreter in my classes, and I had to rely on my hearing as much as possible. Speech therapy was helpful because it helped me to speak clearly and made sure I could say certain sounds. I could not say high frequency sounds clearly because I could not hear them (S's, Ch's, Th's, and Sh's). Being in mainstreamed classes and taking speech therapy helped prepare me for the real world. The school district was also preparing me for the real world, although I did not know it then.

The other thing that was a problem in Oakland was the students in the hard of hearing program were minorities. Their parents or guardians were not probably aware of the power they had over the district because of their lack of education or employment.

> "From the language and implications of Public Law 94-142 (see Appendix), it is obvious that parents will have to play a major role in taking the initiative and leading the attack to ensure that equal educational opportunities for their child are made a reality. Our assumption is that many Black deaf students, parents, and school personnel are not fully aware of the law, its provisions, and its implications . . . Only a few Black parents have the time and resources to vigorously pursue their rights and those of their handicapped children" (30, Hairston and Smith).

Together, parents could have demanded the district help their children or could have sued because the district was not doing its job. My mother was one of the parents who did not know what could have been offered to me. I wanted an FM, but the school did not provide it. They claimed I did not need it, and they did not have the money for it. My audiologist at Children's Hospital had to write a report on the things I needed in school, such as the FM system because she determined that with the FM system, I could have been doing a lot better. Since Oakland Unified School District (OUSD) was not doing its job, my audiologist told my mother to try to get me in Berkeley schools. Berkeley could provide the resources I needed. The problem was we did not know anyone who lived in Berkeley, so we could use their address to get me into the school. Since we were out of options, we had no choice but to put up with Oakland's schools. This was the real world because it was like this almost everywhere when there were urban schools overpopulated with minorities. School districts did not have enough money to improve the schools, and the minorities tended to do worse because they felt as if they were in jail, rather than an academic institution. The teachers had to buy the supplies with their money, and the students did not get adequate textbooks. They had to use outdated books, which did not encourage the students.

Most of the students in my class were either doing remedial work or doing challenging work. The students who did the challenging work were teased because they were seen as trying to be better than the others. I was one of the students who was teased because I could do work beyond my level, and I could hear better than most of them. In the deaf culture, hard of hearing or people that do not have severe hearing loss, are looked down upon because they are seen as trying to deny who they are. It is the same as the African American culture where the light skinned are more favored than the dark skinned, and the light skinned tend to deny their African American culture. I had a hard time trying to fit in the deaf world because I did not know ASL very well, but I could still sign enough to communicate with deaf people. It was not hard trying to do well in school, even with being rejected by my peer group, because I did not let them stop me from getting my education. It made me want to leave Oakland to go to school elsewhere because it was ridiculous trying to excel in school with people trying to pull me down (the crab in the barrel theory).

Not much later, my wish came true. In the middle of fourth grade, my family moved to Berkeley, and I was able to get into Berkeley schools. I finally went to John Muir elementary, which was the school that provided the resources for the deaf students. In Berkeley, the deaf population was smaller than the population in Oakland. In fact, the total number of deaf students in the Berkeley program was about twenty-five students where in Oakland there were a total of possibly one hundred students (from pre-kindergarten to high school). That was a huge difference in terms of how the students were able to get their resources. Berkeley has a population of 59.2% whites (60,797), while the black population is 13.6% (14,007). The Asians are the second highest while the other minorities are lower than blacks in the population of Berkeley (Bay Area Census). Also, in Berkeley the parents are usually middle/ upper class whites. They are more likely to know how much power they have over the school district. Thanks to the Berkeley program being smaller and being in a setting of middle/ upper class whites, I was able to get my FM system and was able to perform better in school.

Although there were two biracial girls, I was the only black student in my class. It was hard for me to adapt since I was coming from an all minority deaf program to a majority white deaf program. I felt alone because no one understood where I was coming from, a ghetto in Oakland. Some of the students lived in Oakland, but they lived in the white areas; so, they did not have any idea what it was like being black in Oakland. I felt more tied to my black community because I was trying to educate the other students what it was like to be black. I observed where they lived (in the Berkeley Hills or by the Claremont Hotel) and compared it to where I lived (South Berkeley, with majority of black people in my neighborhood). We were coming from different areas of Berkeley to go to one school, and I continued to notice patterns. They had more assistants/ interpreters in Berkeley where we had a few in Oakland. We were doing work of our level while the students in Oakland were doing remedial work. The Berkeley parents were doctors, lawyers and writers while the parents in Oakland were often on welfare, SSI, and those who had jobs were not as professional as the ones in Berkeley.

These things I observed made me think for a long time about why the deaf students in Berkeley succeeded in school while the black/ minorities in Oakland were dropping out or not getting an education further than high school. From my observation and experiences, the majority of the students in Berkeley went to California School for the Deaf in Fremont (CSD) after they graduated from John Muir elementary and after CSD, they went to Gallaudet University (a deaf college in Washington DC) or other colleges. The ones in Oakland tended to go to the junior colleges or vocational schools after they graduated from Skyline High school. This led to my research interest: what factors affect educational access for the hearing impaired and how they perform in school, and why does it work for Berkeley but not too well for Oakland? These are important questions to ask and to do research on because there is not a lot of information on deaf children and education, especially comparing whites and minorities. I plan to interview two of my former teachers from both school districts and get data because this is a serious issue to observe and discuss. African American children are already not performing well in schools and the minority deaf/ hard of hearing deaf students are not doing too well themselves. I wanted to look at this issue and try to understand why it is happening so we can try to close the education gap between blacks and whites, and particularly between the black and white hearing impaired students.

LITERATURE REVIEW

There were various articles and books I read that were related to my topic when I first started my research. I was focusing on race and socio-economic status and how they affect students of color in education. Even though I changed my thesis from *Students of Color in Education* to *Deaf Students of Color*, I was going to use some of the books that were related to the concept of what I was discussing. However, after I did the interviews, my focus shifted because some of the books were no longer relevant to my topic. Instead, I had to use the books and articles that were connected to black deaf students and how parents and teachers can help improve their academic achievement.

In *Black and Deaf in America: Are We that Different*, Ernest Hairston and Linwood Smith discussed the history of deaf culture in the African American community and what some of the issues that were being debated. In a chapter, which focused on education, the authors demonstrated how things have changed or remained the same for deaf children who were people of color. This book helped me to comprehend why deaf black children or people are or were not making progress in America's society. Hairston and Smith stated:

"The answer here can be two-pronged in that families on different socio-economic levels face things differently. As mentioned earlier, many Black families are usually burdened with making ends meet, raising a family, and coping with the ever changing world. They generally do not have sufficient time or energy to devote to the deaf child" (7).

"When we expect little of deaf children, most likely we will get little, and when we expect a lot, chances are

we will get a lot. Because the child is deaf is no reason
to have low expectations of their abilities and capabilities" (7).

These two quotes explained what were occurring in some black
families who had deaf children and why black deaf children may not
be succeeding in school. This is related to my thesis because I am
discussing some of the deaf students from Oakland schools who may
have experienced these situations at home or at school. Although one
black parent demonstrated that it was not always true, the fact is it
happened. Still there were other black families who were helping
their children. We cannot stereotype that this happens in every black
family.

*The Black and Deaf Movements in America Since 1960: Parallelism
and an Agenda for the Future,* by Rittenhouse, Johnson, Overton, Freeman, and Jaussi compared how the deaf movement was related to the
Civil Rights Movement. It discussed the things African American deaf
people needed to do to be recognized, as opposed to being ignored.
It discussed every aspect of the African American deaf culture, from
family to education and jobs and how should things improve.

This book emphasized how parents of disabled children or regular
children should play an important role in education. They should not
simply accept whatever the teacher or administration say is right for
their child.

"Under Public Law 94-142 (see Appendix), educational planning, in addition to requiring an individual
analysis of the child's unique educational needs, was to
be characterized by "parent involvement". Parents were
accorded a vital role as active participants in the educational decisions and plans affecting their children, from
initiating and protesting referrals through challenging the appropriateness of programs and placement...
In short, for the first time in history, educators were
required by law to fully inform and work with coopera-
tively with parents, who were to be a part of the educational structure serving their children" (393).

This is one of the most important things the interviewees emphasized: how parent participation is important in every child's learning

because the parents and teachers have to be a team. The children are with the parents longer than they are with the teachers so the parents have to educate their children along with the teachers. It is hard for the teachers to do it in six hours of the day. This was one of the key components of what makes a child successful in school.

Joslyn Martin and Hugh Prickett discussed in *Black Deaf Children: Culture and Education*, how can parents of deaf children become involved with their children and the comparisons between the white families and the black families with deaf children. The white families were more likely to have the resources to communicate with their children and be able to provide their children the resources to get by in life. The black families often were not aware of what can be provided for their children, and they had their own problems to deal with. It was interesting to see the different dynamics people went through when they have children who were deaf, especially when there was a comparison between black and white families.

> "White parents are likely to have access to useful information about deafness from medical personnel, state and local boards of education, and knowledgeable friends and family members. For the family of a white deaf child with no other disabilities, deafness is usually the most important issue the family must deal with" (6).

In my experience, this statement was true for the Berkeley deaf students. The Berkeley deaf students were fortunate because they came from the Center of Education for the Infant Deaf, which is now called Center for Early Intervention on Deafness (CEID), which was how they were able to keep doing well. CEID offered the family sign language classes and other resources for them to use. Since Oakland's deaf students were majority people of color, they probably were not aware of the resources to help their children (since hospitals did not let them know about the variety resources), which could mean that the students went through the education system not doing well.

Ronald Ferguson's *Teacher's Perceptions and Expectations and the Black-White Test Score Gap* discussed how teacher's perceptions affected how students performed in school. It was shown white teachers who had low expectations of black students tended to discourage the students from doing well in school, while they praised the white students' academic performance. These teachers assumed the black students were not capable of doing the school work, so they stereotyped all of their black students as having no potential, while they encouraged the white students to do well.

> "Teachers, like all of us, use the dimensions of class, race, sex, ethnicity to bring order to their perceptions of the classroom environment. Rather than teachers gaining more in-depth and holistic understanding of the child, with the passage of time teachers' perceptions become increasingly stereotyped and children become hardened caricatures of an initially discriminatory vision" (274).

This type of behavior in teachers could also be seen with disabled students. Some teachers believed the disabled students were not capable of doing work beyond their level and tended to keep them at a minimal level. As I will discuss later, this happened to me when I was in the 6th grade, and sometimes I see it with other students in special education. If the teacher has negative perceptions of their students that sometimes can lower the students' self-esteem and lower their academic achievements. Another book that was similar to Ronald Ferguson's is *Deaf Plus: A Multicultural Perspective* by Kathee Christensen. One of the chapters I was reading explained how teachers' perceptions of the black deaf students affected their academic performance and what the solutions were to these barriers.

Some books were not close to what I was discussing, and I decided not to include them at all. Some of the articles had little relation to what I am doing but I thought they would be helpful because they were about educational test scores and how to eliminate the black-white test score gap. However, my topic is bigger than eliminating test score gap, and it is more about how to get black students to perform well academically, especially deaf and other special education students. I hope this thesis will open people's eyes about education and how we can make the system better. Many of our students are failing in the educational system and it seems as if education is not a priority to the government anymore.

METHODOLOGY

During the process of my research to find what affected deaf students' academic performances I learned more than I had anticipated, and consequently I had to change the focus of my thesis. To find books on deaf education, I went to the education library at University California, Berkeley where I found a few articles on deaf education. Since I only had a few articles, I asked my former teachers from the Oakland deaf program where I could find books on deaf education, and she said that San Francisco Public Library has a deaf library. At the San Francisco Public deaf library, I was able find a variety of books and articles on deaf education, particularly focusing on black and white deaf students. I was able to check out the books but not the articles, so I had to photocopy them.

The books and articles I read about black and white deaf students repeatedly asserted certain basic reasons why black deaf students tended not to do as well as the white deaf students. The authors[1] stated that white students often came from wealthier families than black students, and the white families had more resources to give their children a better education. From those statements and arguments, I formed my interview questions based on what I read with the idea of confirming or refuting the statements.

While in the process of reading the books and articles, I had to find interviewees who would be willing to help my research. Some

---

[1]   Martin, Joslyn; Prickett, Hugh; *Black Deaf Children: Culture and Education*; Perspectives, V. 10, No. 1; 1992

2 Hairston, Ernest; Smith, Linwood; *Black & Deaf in America: Are we that Different*; 1993

people backed out because they were afraid to lose their job while others were very willing to help me understand what factors were involved. Since I was comparing my old deaf programs in Oakland and Berkeley, I was able to ask my former teachers and their assistants if they would be willing to do the interview. Luckily, the majority said yes, and some of them referred me to more people who would be willing to help me. Initially, I was not thinking of interviewing the parents of the deaf students because I thought it was just the people in education who could have an impact on what I wanted to understand. After talking to some of my colleagues about my research, they argued I should incorporate the parents' opinions because they are the people who have to make decisions for their children, and they can give me a better understanding of what they had to do for their children. The teachers are not in the homes, and they only know by what they have observed or in the reports. I asked my former teachers if they would be willing to ask some parents if they were interested in being interviewed for my research. Two parents agreed.

I interviewed two teachers (one from each school district), two interpreters (one from each school district), two parents (both from the Berkeley program), and one teacher who worked in Berkeley and Oakland schools. Following are the questions I asked the teachers and assistants that worked with the deaf students.

- What factors, in your experience, improve a student's chance of doing well in school? Why or why not? Any other factors? What factors, in your experience, limit a student's chance of doing well? Why or why not?
- How many of your students go on to college, whether it is a University or a junior college? Why do you think that they do or do not go on to college?
- How many students of color do you have and how many white students do you have?
- Do you think there is an education gap between the black and white students, whether they are deaf or hearing? Why or why not? (I want to hear a teacher's perspective, not a book's).
- How involved are the parents with their children's education? Do they know sign language to communicate with their children? How long have the parents been signing with their children?

The questions I asked the parents were modified so they could demonstrate their perspective as a parent. I asked them what factors improve or limit a student's chances of doing well. But the questions afterwards were changed. Such as:

- Will their children go to college?
- How and when did you find out your child was deaf? What hospital was your child born in and how did you find out what services would help your child?
- When did you learn sign language?

All seven interviewees helped broaden my perspective on the issues in deaf education. Some refuted what the books and articles stated and some confirmed what I have read. Since I learned new things from the interviewees, I changed the focus of my thesis. I initially thought the factors were race and class, but in reality class was most important because there were middle class black parents who did help their children get an excellent education. After reviewing everything the interviewees stated, I felt I had a strong argument for the paper. If I had not interviewed the parents, I would have been biased and that was not my intention. My intention was to gather as much information as possible so I could try to close the educational gap.

My finding was that it was not just black or people of color deaf students who have this problem but hearing students as well. I chose deaf education because it was easier for me to write about my experiences, and there was not a lot of publishing on deaf education and I want to contribute to it. I want people to be aware that there are problems within the deaf educational system and it needs to be fixed along with the other educational problems. It is not just a matter of race but class as well because of the different resources that are available to a particular group of people.

DATA ANALYSIS

Children can become deaf in many ways. Some are born deaf or have complications at birth, they have been ill (fever or diseases), and some are genetic. I lost my hearing at birth because my umbilical cord was wrapped around my neck and caused a lack of oxygen. However, I was fortunate because the doctors were able to tell my mother I either had brain damage or a hearing loss within a few weeks of my birth. They tested me and saw that there was no damage to my brain, but the hearing tests revealed I lost some of my hearing. To test babies on their hearing, they put sensors on the baby's head, and the baby has to wear earphones that have various levels of sounds coming out. If the baby can hear the sounds, the brain will send impulses demonstrating the nerves are reacting to it.

However, some parents do not find out their child is deaf until about the age of 15 months, when the average hearing child begins to speak. Both of the parents I interviewed expressed how they noticed their child was not speaking or responding to certain noises. As one Berkeley parent expressed,

> "My daughter was born deaf and we (she and her husband) found out when she was 17 months old. I had my daughter's hearing tested right away on the first day of pre-school, because I saw that my daughter wasn't speaking. The pre-school teacher asked me if I had her hearing tested and that was when I tested her right away."

Another Berkeley parent found out through someone else in the family her son was deaf. She said,

> "I found out he was deaf through my great-grandmother because my great-grandmother knew something

wasn't right. I took him to Kaiser (the hospital where he was born) so they could perform the tests on him, and he didn't wake up from the noises or get signals from the ABR that mean that his nerves can hear the sounds."

It was interesting to see it took someone else in the family or school to tell the parents their child was deaf or needed to have their hearing tested. Both parents sensed something was wrong with their child because they were not speaking around the time when the average hearing child speaks. It took an outsider to recognize and confirm what the parents sensed. The good thing was the parents listened to what people suggested to them, and they took their children to the doctor. Sometimes they wondered how their child knew when someone was home if they could not hear anything. One of the parents explained she figured her son used his vision to enhance what he could not hear. She explained the curtains moved when someone opened the door, so that was how her son knew when his father was home.

After the parents took their child to the doctor, the tests revealed their child was deaf, and the doctors referred them to places that specialized in deaf children. As Ernest Hairston and Linwood Smith explained in their book, *Black and Deaf in America: Are We that Different*:

> "Most medical doctors after determining a hearing loss in their child then refer parents to an audiologist. The audiologist is trained in the non-medical measurement of hearing loss and prescribes hearing ads and rehabilitation."(5)

Children's Hospital in North Oakland was probably the best place in the Bay Area to go for children with special needs, especially hearing needs. The parents who were interviewed and my mother went to Children's Hospital because the audiologists referred them to good schools, advised them on what was best for the child and provided the best hearing aids. The audiologist referred the parents to Center of Education for the Infant Deaf (CEID) in North Berkeley, where the children and parents could learn sign language and get the services they needed for their child to do well in school. A teacher in Berkeley for the deaf program explained that:

"CEID helps the families and help the parents to learn sign language. Early beginnings or early education from CEID helps make a difference. It's not an economic issue, it's an issue of are parents aware of the services provided for their children at an early age (Children's Hospital refer parents to CEID, Kaiser [hospital] doesn't). CEID is a public institution and people who live outside of Berkeley can still attend CEID. Again, it's a matter of who is informed of what is out there for their children."

When the interviewee mentioned the hospitals and the differences between them, I began to ask the parents where their children were born. One of the parents said her son was born in Kaiser, but Kaiser did not specialize in hearing tests, they performed the basics to see if the child could hear. Fortunately, they referred her to Children's Hospital otherwise she would have been trying to enroll her son in a deaf program that had a waiting list, whereas, CEID did not have a waiting list. When she enrolled her son in CEID, he felt as if he was at "home" because he was in an environment where he could communicate with other people. She said that "he went to CEID since Children's told us of a deaf program that didn't have a waiting list. Once he got to CEID, he started signing and we learned sign language together. So, we've been signing since he was about 15-18 months." Another Berkeley mother said, "I started signing when my daughter went to CEID, and I hired a private tutor for signing classes (she had sign language classes twice a week)."

Both of the parents praised CEID and everything that the school had done for their children and the family. They were able to catch up with their children by signing and communicating with their children. In an article, *Recommended Practices in Family Involvement*, the authors discussed how programs for children with special needs can help the families understand their child's disability and what services may be good for them. Even though this program was in Los Angeles, California, it was similar to CEID's program.

"...Services support language and communication. These services-home sign language or parenting classes held on site or in the community-may be written in the family's Individualized Family Service Plan, the document

that is required for very young children with disabilities...
In addition, the program offers the opportunity for infor-
mal gatherings and workshops to address to community
social services and health care... Parents and caregivers
also receive support from the Infant Services audiologists
and speech therapists who meet with families in their
home or in group meetings." (*Odyssey*, 8)

CEID offered similar programs for the parents and families; so, the
parents could get the attention they needed to understand their child's
deafness. This program was similar to the Individualized Education
Plan because it is a document that is required for all special education
students. Parents need a support group because they can learn what
may or may not work for their child since every child has different
needs. CEID helped the parents learn what was good for their child,
especially at an early age. They would always know what their child's
weaknesses and strengths were in the beginning, and they could follow through until the children were older to make their own decision
about what worked for them and what did not. The parents in Berkeley were fortunate they caught their child's hearing loss at an early
age, even though to them, it was later than when hearing children
started talking. They were able to get the support system they needed
to make sure their child excelled academically.

It is critical for parents to find out early on if their child is deaf
because children learn their language at home before the pre-school
age. "Early profound deafness is said to be the most severe handicap
a child can have because he is denied the most vital developmental
stimulus of all- the voice" (9, Hairston and Smith). Since the parents
found out early on, they were able to recover most of the language
development with their child and get their child ready for pre-school.
Their child was at a pre-school that used sign language and the children were able to learn how to communicate. *The Black and Deaf
Movements in America Since 1960* stated, "Without adequate communication, hearing impaired children are deprived of an essential support system-the family..." (395). Communication with the child is very
important otherwise a deaf child would be missing a lot of vital information and would be frustrated. Similar to how the mother's son felt
"at home" at his pre-school because he found a way to communicate

with his family and vice versa. Also, by having a television that had closed caption (words on the television), the child could learn how to read and get their language development from television. Deaf students tended to read better when they had close captioned on their television because they were constantly learning new vocabulary.

In most cases, class is connected to parent participation because a family that is wealthy can provide better services for their children. For instance, one family in Berkeley, which consists of a doctor and a writer, was able to hire a private tutor for sign language who came to their house once a week. They had two classes, one at CEID, and the other at their house because they wanted to be able to communicate with their daughter. Also, they were able to buy books on deaf culture and how to raise a deaf child and get the help they needed to make sure everyone was comfortable with their situation. They are able to buy multiple televisions for their home that had closed caption built inside of it (the box for closed caption that you hook up to the television, were no longer available). Some parents could not afford to buy a new television with closed caption built inside, which could have an effect on their children's reading level. In addition, with the parents' college education and beyond, they were able to research their rights and fight for what was right for their child. Although the family was Jewish, there was a connection with an article titled, *Black Deaf Children: Culture and Education.*

> "White parents are likely to have access to useful information about deafness from medical personnel, state and local boards of education, and knowledgeable friends and family members. For the family of a white deaf child with no other disabilities, deafness is usually the most important issue the family must deal with" (Martin and Prickett, 6).

Not to say this is a racial issue but in some cases, this is true. However, there are black parents who are able to have access to information about deafness and their child's rights as well.

In special education, there is a legal contract called Individualized Education Plan (IEP), in which the parents, teachers and school administration congregate once a year about what the child needs and how have they improved on their weaknesses. As I stated earlier, the

IEP is a legal document, which states what the students need in order to perform well in school. The important member of the IEP is the parent because they can decide what is right for their child and learn ways to help improve their child's weaknesses and strengths. "Parents were accorded a vital role as active participants in the educational decisions and plans affecting their children, from initiating and protesting referrals through challenging the appropriateness of programs and placements" (Rittenhouse, 339). It is no longer the teacher's job to tell the parents what their child needs but the parent's job too because they have to be a team to make sure that the child is successful in school. If the school does not provide the services, the parents can fight the district because the district is mandated to provide the services, which shows that parents are involved in their children's education because they know what necessities the child is supposed to have in school.

Most parents that come from the middle-upper classes will know their rights and how to fight the educational system, if they are not satisfied with their children's services. In contrast, lower class and people of color are not informed of their rights, such as the parents of deaf children in Oakland.

> "No law is a good law unless it is enforced. From the language and implications of Public Law 94-142, it is obvious that parents will have to play a major role in taking the initiative and leading the attack to ensure that equal educational opportunities for their child are made a reality. Our assumption is that many Black deaf students, parents, and school personnel are not fully aware of the law, its provisions, and its implications ...Only a few Black parents have the time and resources to vigorously pursue their rights and those of their handicapped children" (Hairston and Smith, 30).

When I attended Oakland's deaf program, there was a higher number of deaf students (there were the pre-school, elementary, middle and high school students) than Berkeley, especially students of color. In addition, the deaf programs in Oakland were not adequate for the students, and the students seemed to be further behind than the students in Berkeley, and they still are. Most of the deaf students came from families that were in poverty, foster care or extended families. As an Oakland teacher stated,

> "The most important thing is family support, extended family, they must sign and support the children. Students tend not to do well because of broken families, foster care, families who have experienced hardships for various reasons and very few sign. They need language support; no language development at home affects their abilities in school. Hearing kids or deaf kids that sign at home, have that full experience of the world that deaf kids in an oral environment doesn't get the socialization and vocabulary development, which is an enthusiasm for learning."

Additionally, these were the same students whose parents do not sign to them, either because they had to work or there was not enough time and money to learn sign language, such as my mother. Although my mother did not sign, she was middle class, and she still read to me and educated me so I was able to develop my language. Some deaf students grew up in an oral environment (without signing) where their parents were involved, and they still performed well academically. "Families that don't sign make education important for their children, which is why those students tend to do well because they are ready and willing [due to family support]," said an Oakland teacher. The children whose parents were not involved with their learning process were usually the children who had trouble learning at school. The lack of language or lack of interacting at home set the children back at a lower educational level where they had to "catch-up" to the hearing students all their life. In regards to the IEP, the IEP guideline book is handed to the parents at every IEP meeting, but the words are in legal terms that lower class people cannot understand. This can affect the students' education because the parents do not know they can fight the school district if they are not satisfied with their children's education.

Another issue is students in poverty have a hard time trying to focus in school because they have not eaten, or they do not have hearing aids. A teacher from Bret Harte Middle School expressed how she had to worry more about the children's health rather than if they had their hearing aids because nutrition was more important in order to function at school. This was obviously related to class because money buys food, which is a necessity for people to do better at school or work. Also, because most of the students were in foster care, sometimes the foster parents did not know sign language to communicate with the children because it was usually a temporary situation.

Although class is related to how students perform in school, race is not always the issue. As a Berkeley mother expressed,

> "A middle class black family can have the resources for their children to perform well academically and encourage the notion that education is important. A poor white family may not have the resources for their children to do well because of where they live and the type of education and jobs they have. So, that put them at a disadvantage while the middle class blacks are at an advantage."

She was right, race was not always an issue but class was. Families have a huge impact on their children's education. If a family has a college degree and beyond, they are likely to instill in their children that education is important. For example, a Berkeley teacher's assistant said, "I think the expectations are different (for deaf children), if the family has education themselves [then] they have their mind set. [They] lead their children to think they are going to college." In addition, a teacher in Berkeley said, "Educational level in families is another factor for the education gap because without the parents that have some education level, the children don't do well because they aren't taught that education is important." My mother did not graduate from college, she had some form of higher education, and she always told me school comes first. I was raised knowing education was important, and schoolwork came before any other activities. Although class can affect educational achievements, some families can be in poverty and still teach their children that education is important. As an interviewee who worked in Berkeley and Oakland expressed, "Yes, the family is involved, but that doesn't excuse the discrepancy between their educational opportunities. Children from poor families do have the potential to do well in school. I think our society, as a whole is responsible for this situation." Families do have an impact on a student's academic achievement since they are the people who raise the child and teach them what is important in their family. If a family values money more than an education, then the students may value money more than their education. In the media, black entertainers are always presented in rich, materialistic items, which show you can be an athlete or a rapper to make a lot of money or raise your status. Black children do not see many black professionals on television, and if their family emphasizes the importance of money through playing sports or rapping then how will they know that getting an education can help them make money too.

Parents or family members have to encourage their children to get an education and tell them the benefits of having a diploma from anything beyond high school. However, parents cannot do it all alone. They may need support from the teachers, who work with their children and help them develop their child's interest in school. *The Black and Deaf Movements in America since 1960...* states,

> "It is believed that they (families) can influence virtually every aspect of school life, including what is taught and how, the way students are treated, and the policies determining promotion and graduation... Indelicato has summarized the benefits that accrue when families and educators work together: students do better in school; teachers have fewer problems with students and report greater satisfaction with students' work; parents have more positive feelings about the school and themselves and are more likely to support school programs; and the community is more apt to offer financial and moral support for school based efforts" (395).

This statement was a strong support of what I stated above. Families can have an influence on the students' lives and can guide them through what is right and wrong, and they can get support from the teachers. Then again, teachers need support from the parents, too. A teacher from Oakland said, "I don't get the kind of support at the home that will improve child's abilities to succeed in school. They need language support; no language development at home affects their abilities in school."

> "Communication within the family, parent involvement, and school programs that matches the expectations and foundations that the parents started at home. School

and parents have to be a good match because if the school
doesn't have the same expectations as the parents, then
the kids may tend to not do well. School and parents have
to reinforce each other" (Berkeley and Oakland teacher).

Many of the interviewees that worked in schools said the notion
of parents and teachers working together are significant in academic
achievement. This showed how important parent involvement and
teacher involvement was when working with children who had special
needs and who did not have special needs because parents and teachers have to emphasize the importance of education. If one or the other
is not working together, then the student may lack an interest in school
because someone is not trying to help them or show them that they care.

Teachers for the deaf have to have an open mind when they teach
deaf children. They need to have experience in signing for more than
two years, be knowledgeable about how to work with deaf students
and the deaf culture. Teachers should not just teach deaf students
about deaf culture but hearing students too, if they are in a mainstreamed program. As a Berkeley interpreter emphasized, "Schools
should teach positive things about deafness and interaction with the
hearing. Schools [should] teach sign language [or] set up a sign club,
encouraging students to sign." Most of all, teachers must have high
expectations and positive perceptions of the students. It is noted when
teachers are positive about their students' academic performance, the
students tend to do better than when the teachers are negative, especially in deaf education.

"Deaf kids at John Muir have an advantage because
in some of their special education classes there are more
one on one, more support and higher expectations, more
learning explanations more in depth explanations and
full understanding from the teacher how to present education in a visual way" (Berkeley interpreter).

Deaf students need to feel they are able to do anything like the
hearing students and, their hearing loss is not a factor preventing
them from excelling in school. However, if teachers keep putting them
down and limiting their ability, then the students could feel as if they
cannot do challenging work. In *Teacher's Expectations and the Test
Score Gap*, it states:

"Teachers, like all of us, use the dimensions of class, race, sex, ethnicity to bring order to their perception of the classroom environment. Rather than teachers gaining more in-depth and holistic understanding of the child, with the passage of time teachers' perceptions become increasingly stereotyped and children become hardened caricatures of an initially discriminating vision" (Ferguson, 274).

This also goes with disability because some teachers can believe that disabled or students with special needs cannot do challenging work or do work on their grade level. Kathee Christensen wrote in *Deaf Plus: A Multicultural Perspective*, "Teacher attitudes and perceptions of their students, more specifically students of color, are important in the level of expectations set for their students and in the kind of treatment these students receive in their classrooms" (257). In addition to Christensen's quote, an Oakland interpreter stated, "Having good teachers, teachers that can see that every child has capabilities and see past previous negative records and trying to get past their prejudice and biases" is important for deaf students and students of color to excel in school.

From personal observations, I noticed the teachers at John Muir challenged their students and gave them work that was at their level or beyond. They encouraged their students to interact with everything in the school community, such as take them to stores so the deaf students could learn how to communicate with hearing people. At Bret Harte, some of the students are 6th-8th graders, and they were doing 3rd grade level or lower level work because it seemed as if no one pushed them when they were younger; some students seemed to have been lost in the system. This showed that teachers have to help prepare the students for the world as well as the parents because they work hand in hand. "When we expect little of deaf children, most likely we will get little, and when we expect a lot, chances are we will get a lot. Because the child is deaf is no reason to have low expectations of their abilities and capabilities" (Hairston and Smith, 7). Teachers have to believe their students are capable and encourage them because sometimes they may not get encouraged at home.

For example, I had a teacher for the deaf in 6th grade, and I was the only student in his class (there was another hard of hearing student but she did not take his class). He tended to put me down and say I would never amount to anything in life. The work he assigned me was below my level, and I did worse in school because that lowered my self-esteem. Although my mother encouraged me to do well, the teacher's perceptions of me made me feel as if I was not good enough to excel academically. In contrast, when I went to the 7th grade, my grades improved two times more because I had teachers who encouraged me and believed I was capable of doing "regular" work. Teachers' attitudes reflect on the students and can have an impact on their performance in school.

Another thing I have noticed between the two schools was John Muir had the speech therapists take the students out of the school to have them practice their speech. The parents signed a permission slip allowing the students to go off campus to a nearby store to practice ordering their food and test their ability to communicate with the hearing world. Thanks to the teachers and speech therapists exposing them to the world, the students were able to feel confident about asking for help and ordering their food without feeling ashamed. One of the Berkeley mothers explained how one of the deaf students went on a field trip with California School for the Deaf in Fremont and how the teachers did not recognize she was not present in the group. The girl fell asleep on BART (a local subway in the Bay Area), and when she woke up she was in San Francisco and started to cry because she was alone. However, she "snapped" out of it and started to think, "What should I do?" She went to the information desk for BART and explained she was deaf, and she needed to go to Fremont. The person told her to get on the Fremont train. She found her way back to the school, and she was proud that she had that exposure of knowing what to do in a situation like this.

I remember when I was in Oakland, we rarely took public transportation for field trips because some of the parents chaperoned, and we rode in cars. The speech therapists in Oakland did not take us to nearby stores to practice our communication skills. We practiced in her office and hoped that we learned something out of it. In Berkeley, it was easy to know we made a mistake because sometimes the clerks would ask us to repeat our orders, and we would rephrase it to make them understand us better. Then the speech therapists would tell us afterwards why we had to repeat ourselves or would tell us good job on rephrasing our orders.

Berkeley taught the students how to communicate and "get around," so they would not feel helpless in some situations. Often times, Oakland did not have field trips with public transportation because sometimes the students could not afford the bus or train fare, and the teachers had to use their money to help the students. They had to teach their students what to do in the classrooms as opposed to going into the outside world. School is not just about academic knowledge but "street" knowledge too because schools have to teach you how to use what you learned in the class outside of the classroom.

This is a perfect example of a school working together with the parents because the schools have to enforce what the parents teach at home, such as being social in the world. Parents educate their children at home and teachers educate the children at school to make sure the students are prepared for the real world. They work hand in hand. The teachers and parents have to make sure the students are getting enough exposure, especially deaf students. If parents do not tell the teachers what they want for their child in the IEP, then it is hard for the teachers to know what works best for the students. Every student is different, and it takes more than one person to raise a child to be successful in school and in work. There is a saying, "It takes a village to raise a child," and that statement is true. Everyone has to contribute to make sure a child is productive in society because everyone has his or her own specialty.

As I observed the different factors that affect deaf children's academic performance, I realized how biased I was before I interviewed the teachers and parents. I thought the biggest issue was race and class when that was not always the case. I learned class was an important issue, but it was also about parent involvement and supportive teachers. These two sets of people can make a huge impact on children's education because it takes encouragement and motivation to do well in school. Although Bret Harte has supportive teachers, it is hard to keep a child enthusiastic about school when they are having trouble at home (family and financial problems). As a teacher from Bret Harte expressed, "It is hard to teach students who are dealing with life issues (drug addiction, neglect, and abuse) and who do not value education. Some parents do not value education; so, the children are raised not to value it." As Martin and Prickett stated, "The education of black deaf children must rely on concerned teachers, parents, and others who vigorously demand quality educational programs and maximum results for each individual child. Black deaf children deserve no less" (24).

> "If we can try to begin to address the cultural needs of every minority student and that teachers are attempting to become more sensitive and their expectations of these kids become higher and with more parent involvement and more multicultural-environment acceptance, then, I believe, these kids can achieve more than they are now, along with more Black Deaf and Black Professionals" (*Deaf Life*, 14).

Teachers and parents have to work together in order for children to succeed in school because there needs to be a strong foundation for the students to rely on.

Also, the education gap needs to be narrowed or closed because it causes friction in deaf education. Again, race is not always a factor of why deaf students of color do not perform well academically; class is the main issue. Middle and upper class families are able to buy books and computers to educate their children, while some poor or working class families cannot. In addition, middle class and beyond can buy the best hearing aids and get the best services for their children while some have to struggle with what they have. Many of the teachers or interpreters that I have interviewed explained money was an issue in terms of the educational gap because the money provides food, clothes, necessities, and books to keep the mind functioning and expanding. When you are poor, you have trouble learning because you do not have the proper food, clothes and necessities to stay focused. Family background is a key factor in educational gaps because when you come from a family that has education beyond high school, it tends to have a positive impact on children's education because the parents can help with the homework and can help educate their children.

CONCLUSION

With regard to what can be done to improve academic success of deaf students, my findings revealed the importance of parent involvement and dedicated teachers. Parents need to understand the small things they do (such as, sign, read to them using sign language, interact with them) makes a huge impact in their children's lives. By communicating in sign language and reading to their children with sign language, they are helping their children's language development. Children learn at home before they go to pre-school or school. By the time their children go to pre-school, they know how to communicate. They are able to learn the alphabet and how to read.

It is the parents' responsibility to make sure they get the services they need for the children once they find out their children are deaf. Sometimes deafness does not get detected until the child is 15 months, around the age when hearing children tend to talk. The parents need to go to the doctor, so their child can get tested. The parents also have to do their own research about services for their deaf child because some hospitals will not offer solutions or will not refer the parents to other places that specialize in deaf children/ deaf education or services. Sometimes if the parents wait until their child gets into school to learn sign language, the child's language skills are less developed than those whose parents signed to them since they were babies. Children learn language fast, and if they learn sign language at home, by the time they go to school they are not behind.

However, not many parents know their children learn from them first before they learn outside of the home. Parents from the lower class are not always home because they are working two jobs or working long hours, especially if they have no education beyond high school or no high school diploma. There should be programs to help parents who do not have a college degree, so they can help their children. People with college degrees or education beyond high school tend to educate their children by buying books and reading to them (using sign language), and they push for their education at home so when they go to school they are caught up or ahead. Parents with education beyond high school tend to make more money and have resources to help their children (tutoring, after school programs, learning technology and computers). It is not a matter of race but a matter of class. A middle class black family could have more resources to help their children do well in school than a poor white family that does not have the resources to help their children perform better.

Additionally, teachers need to be supportive of their students because teachers' expectations and perceptions of their students affect the students' performance. If teachers have low expectations and negative perceptions then the students feel as if they do not have to try since the teachers already have their minds set. If students do not try, then their grades drop, especially in deaf education. Teachers of deaf students need to have high expectations and positive perceptions so their students feel as if they accepted and capable. Teachers need to teach their students about deaf culture and their language (American Sign Language) because that enforces positive identification with the deaf culture. Also, by the students using sign language and other forms of communication that helps them to do better in school because they are not missing anything and they are getting the information they need.

Schools that have deaf programs need to educate hearing students about deafness and give them signing classes so they can communicate with deaf students. From my experiences and observations, when the school is not teaching hearing student's sign language, it tends to isolate the deaf students and make them feel inferior to the hearing students. When hearing students sign, deaf students do not feel they are looked down upon, and they are able to participate in conversations or activities with hearing students. Also, teachers who encourage field trips with deaf students help them learn how to socialize with hearing people who do not know how to sign. By having the students practice their speech or communication skills, the students learn they are not disabled and can communicate with hearing people. They learn confidence in being able to tell someone they are deaf, and the person may need to slow down or write things down. They do not feel ashamed to say they are deaf.

In order to understand how educational success is achieved, you have to look at the factors that impact children in school. Everyone has different opinions about how is children's success is achieved but in my research, most of the readings and interviewees were in agreement: parent participation and background are the most important factors as well as the academic institution itself. Both need to help each other because teachers cannot always do it by themselves, and parents cannot do it by themselves (although sometimes they can) because they go hand in hand. The parents and teachers have to help prepare the deaf students to function in the real/hearing world. The students learn confidence within themselves and their peer groups because they are reinforcing deaf pride from the support from their family and school community. Parents need to communicate with the teachers and other deaf specialists to find ways to help their children succeed academically. That is why they have IEP meetings annually so everyone can congregate and decide what is best for the student. They have to be a team and they have to enforce each other, otherwise children will not necessarily get the education they need.

BIBLIOGRAPHY

Zora Neale Hurston: *Their Eyes Were Watching God*; 1937

Lovergirl: the Teena Marie Story, album; 1997

Behind the Groove: Unofficial Teena Marie Page;
http://www.angelfire.com/la/dyt/teena.html

I Need Your Lovin', The Very Best of Teena Marie, album; 1994

James L. Conyers: *African American Jazz and Rap*; 2000

VH-1's *Where Are They Now: Girl Power*; 1999

Teena Marie: Ultimate Collection, album; 2000

www.teenamarie.com

James Oliver Horton and Lois E. Horton: *In Hope of Liberty: Culture, Community and Protest among Northern Free Blacks, 1700-1860*; 1998

Black Migration (author and year unknown)

James L. Conyers: *African American Jazz and Rap*; 2000

Soul Food: TV Series 2000-2004 (Waterworks LLC
• Edmonds Entertainment Group (EEG)
• Paramount Network Television Productions
• Showtime Networks)

Ann Arnett Ferguson: *Bad Boys: Public Schools in the Making of Black Masculinity (Law, Meaning, and Violence)*; 1991

Higher Learning: The movie; John Singleton; 1995

Kenneth O'Reilly: *Racial Matters: The FBI's Secret File on Black America 1960-1972*; 1991

Kathleen Cleaver and George Katsiaficas: *Liberation, Imagination, and the Black Panther Party*; 2001

Assata Shakur and Angela Davis: *Assata: An Autobiography*; 2001

Biggie and Tupac: Produced by Georgea Blakey (executive producer), Barney Broomfield (executive producer); Nick Broomfield (producer), and Michele d'Acosta (produced); 2002

Martha Shirk, Neil Bennett, and J. Lawrence Aber: *Lives on the Line*: American Families And The Struggle To Make Ends Meet; 2000

Michael Omi and Howard Winant: *Racial Formations in the United States:* From the 1960s to the 1990s (Critical Social Thought)' 1994

Ian Lopez: *White By Law: The Legal Construction of Race; 1997*

David Cole: *No Equal Justice: Race and Class in the American Criminal Justice System*; 1999

Ruthie Gilmore: *You Have Dislodged a Boulder: Mothers and Prisoners in the Post Keynesian California Landscape; 1999*

Cheryl Harris; *Whiteness as Property*; 1993

Larvester Gaither: *All the Brother Wanted Was a Ride: Lynching and Police Powers in Texas*; 2000

Kimberle Crenshaw: *The Intersection of Race and Gender; (year unknown)*

Angela Davis: *Racism, Birth Control and Reproductive Rights; 1982*

Dorothy Roberts: *Killing the Black Body:* Race, Reproduction, and the Meaning of Liberty; *1989*

Dinesh D'Souza: *The End of Racism: Principles for a Multiracial Society*; 1995

Charles R. Lawrence III and Mari J. Matsuda: *We Won't Go Back: Making the Case for Affirmative Action; 1997*

Nathalie Augustin: *Learnfare and Motherhood*; (year unknown)

Nada Elia: *A Woman's Place is in the Struggle; (year unknown)*

Soul Food: The Movie: 1997:
Kenneth 'Babyface' Edmonds   ...executive producer
Tracey E. Edmonds   ...producer
Michael McQuarn   ...co-producer
Robert Teitel   ...producer
Llewellyn Wells   ...line producer

Women and The New International Division of Labor (author and year unknown)

Roderick A. Ferguson: *Aberrations in Black: Toward a Queer of Color Critique;* 2003

Thesis Bibliography
Books

Christensen, Kathee; Deaf Plus: A Multicultural Perspective; Dawn Sign Press, 2000

Ferguson, Ronald F.; "Teacher's Perceptions and Expectations and the Black-White Test Score Gap", The Black-White Test Score Gap; N.W., Washington D.C.; Brookings Institution Press; 1998

Hairston, Ernest; Smith, Linwood; Black and Deaf in America: Are We that Different; T.J. Publishers, Inc., 1983

Phillips, Meredith; Brooks-Gunn, Jeanne; Duncan, Greg J.; Klebanov, Pamela; Crane, Jonathan; "Family Background, Parenting Practices, and the Black-White Test Score Gap"; The Black-White Test Score Gap; N.W., Washington D.C.; Brookings Institution Press; 1998

Ramsey, Claire L.; Deaf Children in Public Schools: Placement, Context, and Consequences; Gallaudet University Press; 1997

Articles
"Reginald Redding: An Overwhelming Sense of Commitment"; Deaf Life; April 1991; pg. 10-15

Elliott, Marta; "School Finance and Opportunities to Learn: Does Money Well Spent Enhance Students' Achievement?"; Sociology of Education, Vol. 71; July 1998, pg. 223-245

Martin, Joslyn E.; Prickett, Hugh T.; Black Deaf Children: Culture and Education; pg. 6-8; Perspectives, v. 10, No. 1, March/April 1992.

"Recommended Practices in Family Involvement"; Odyssey; Winter 2002; pg. 8-12

Rittenhouse, Robert; Johnson, Calvin; Overton, Betty; Freeman, Shirley; Jaussi, Kyle; The Black and Deaf Movements in America Since 1960. Parallelism and Agenda for the Future; American Annals of the Deaf; v. 136, No. 5

Websites (in order as they appear in the thesis)
http://where.com/scott.net/asl/abc.html

http://census.abag.ca.gov/cities/Oakland.htm

http://employment.ousd.k12.ca.us/sub_about_district.asp
http://www.scn.org/~bk269/94-142.html
http://asclepius.com/angel/special.html

www.ingramcontent.com/pod-product-compliance
Lightning Source LLC
Chambersburg PA
CBHW070149290526
45789CB00002B/691